M000208769

MEDITERRANEO EDITIONS

Chania

The City & The Prefecture

Text by
STELLA KALOGERAKI
Archaeologist

Layout
VANGELIS PAPIOMYTOGLOU

DTP
NATASA ANTONAKI

Photographs
VANGELIS PAPIOMYTOGLOU, GIORGOS MARKOULAKIS

Translation from Greek into English by
JULIA CRALLI

Co-ordination of translation work:
COM N. PRATSINIS-K. ZISSIMOU PARTNERSHIP
Conference Interpretation & Translation Services
WWW.PRA-ZIS.GR

Printing and Colour Separation
TYPOCRETA

Copyright 2003
MEDITERRANEO EDITIONS
Tel. +3028310 21590, Fax: +3028310 21591

www.mediterraneo.gr

ISBN: 960-8227-24-0

Chania

The City & The Prefecture

C O N T E N T S

4

C O N T E N T S

Chania
ON THE MAP

Chania
city & road map

The Prefecture of Chania occupies the western portion of Crete and encompasses an area of 2,376 square kilometers. The Sea of Crete laps its northern shore and Sea of Libya the southern. It shares its eastern border with

Chania
RETHYMNO
HERAKLEIO
AG. NIKOLAOS
SITIA
IERAPETRA

the Prefecture of Rethymnon. The large peninsulas of

Akrotirion, Rodopos and Gramvoussa, which characterize the northern coastline, form the large gulfs of Kissamos, Chania and Suda. Suda Bay, in fact, is also one of the largest ports on the Mediterranean. Chania, the capital of the prefecture, is a picturesque seaside town with perfectly preserved historical

features, a modern infrastructure, and an active cultural life. Just south of the city lies the massif of the Lefka (White) Mountains. The range extends to the Sea of Libya and covers nearly 1/3 of the area of the prefecture. In addition to the picturesque traditional villages perched on its slopes, the Lefka Mountains are a true

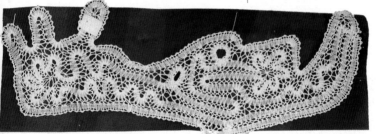

Embroidery depicting Crete

The Samarian Gorge

The wild goat of Crete

nature lover's paradise with dozens of gorges, and numerous ravines, plateaus, rivers and mountain peaks to enjoy. Besides the natural beauty of the landscape itself, you can discover rare species of flora and fauna, and if you're lucky you might even see a wild Cretan ibex, or kri-kri. The region of Sfakia lies on the southern and southeastern part of this mountain range, and has mountains (the highest of which is Pahnes at 2,450 m.),

many ravines, and pristine beaches.

The Samarian Gorge is the major monument to nature in this region. It is not only the largest gorge in Crete but in all of Europe as well and was declared a National Park in 1962. Southwest of Chania is the plain of Kantanos, an area

Chrysoskalitissa

filled with Byzantine churches and historical monuments, the seaside resort of Paleohora, with its fortress and many archeological sites, and the important

cities of ancient Crete: Lissos, Syia, Elyros, and Yrtakina. The region of Kissamos, to the northwest, is teeming with natural and cultural points of interest. Some of these include the rugged landscape of Elafonissi with its amphitheatrical villages dotting the west coast, the traditional villages of Inahorio, the peninsulas of Gramvoussa and Rodopos, and the unique archeological sites of Falassarna, Polyrrinia and Diktynna. In addition, one can find monasteries, Byzantine churches, small ravines, and, of course, wonderful beaches to the east and west of Gramvoussa.

The Lefka (White) Mountains

THE CITY

HISTORY
MONUMENTS
MUSEUMS

HISTORY

Mythology Neolithic & Minoan Periods

Archeological finds provide proof that the area around the city of Chania has been occupied continuously since the Minoan period. Excavations done on Kastelli hill, located just above the harbor, as well as in various spots throughout the modern town, have produced signs of settlement dating back to the late Neolithic period.

Homer frequently refers to Chania as one of the most important cities in Crete. Strabo, the ancient Greek geographer and historian, tells us that King Minos divided Crete into three sections that centered around Kydonia, Knossos, and Gortyn. According to Strabo, the Kydonians were indigenous people and were considered to be the Eteocretans of western Crete.

The early Minoan settlement on Kastelli hill has proved to be the origin of ancient Kydonia. Formal excavations, led by the archeologist Ioannis Tsedakis, began there in 1965. Kastelli hill, as well as sections

uncovered within the city of Chania, contained houses with rooms, hearths, and plastered walls. The hill was without doubt the center of this seaside settlement and, though excavation evidence from the subsequent middle Minoan period is limited, it is certain that it remained so. The late Minoan period marked the settlement's zenith. This was the time when the city was established along a grid plan, the sewer system was developed, and the houses were stately with multiple stories and rooms. A major find dating

Mythology has it that Kydonia was founded by Kydon, the son of Mercury and the nymph Akakkalida, the daughter of King Minos. Mercury, who then went to Mount Olympus, impregnated Akakkalida. The nymph gave birth to Kydon and abandoned him in the mountains where he was raised by animals. Kydon had a daughter, Eulimeni, who was promised as the wife of Apteros, founder of the neighboring city, Aptera. But Eulimeni's clandestine affair with Lycaster delayed her marriage to Apteros. When war broke out between the neighboring cities, Kydon asked the oracle to divine what he must do. The oracle replied that he must sacrifice a virgin. Lots were drawn and the King's own daughter Eulimeni was chosen. After she was sacrificed, she was discovered to be pregnant by Lykaster. Apteros then murdered Lykaster and left the region to settle in Lykia.

10

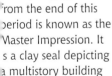

complex by the sea, and horns of consecration, with a dominant male figure above the buildings. By the end of the Late Minoan period, i.e. during the last centuries of the second millennium, city of Chania was flourishing. There are signs of strong Mycenaean influence in all areas of architectural and artistic endeavor. The Linear B tablets discovered in the Greek-Swedish excavations of 1989/ 1990 also date from that period. These documents indicate that the city was most probably a palace-type construction. The prosperity of the late Minoan period abruptly came to an end around the 12th century, when for reason not known most of the settlements, including the city of Chania, were abandoned without any apparent sign of some catastrophe.

from the end of this period is known as the Master Impression. It s a clay seal depicting a multistory building

Section of excavation on Kastelli hill

Gold earrings from the Hellenistic period

Historical Years

The Geometric period dates from the beginning of the first millennium and is primarily characterized by the use of iron, the practice of cremation, and pottery decorated with geometric motifs. The first evidence of the existence of a geometric settlement in the city of Chania dates from the 8th century. Most of the finds are ceramic shards from Kastelli hill. Architectural remains from this period are very limited. Classical Kydonia, whose founding dates from 542 BC, extended south to the Lefka Mountains, east to the Spatha (Psakon) promontory where it bordered with the region of Polyrrinia, and west to Maleha (Kyamon) where it bordered with the dominions of Apteros. According to Herodotus, the city was rebuilt in 519 by the Samians, who had gone there after rebelling against their tyrant, Polycrates. The Samians definitely were not the founders of Kydonia but they did inhabit the already existing region of Minoan Crete, whose location is identified with that of the city of Chania. The new city was built on top of the ancient and classical cities, and this is why there are so few architectural remains from these earlier settlements in contrast to the impressive quantity and quality of the portable finds. It is interesting to note that the sculptor Krissilas, the pupil of the famous sculptor Phidias, came from Kydonia. Also noteworthy is the fact that during the Peloponnesian War, the Athenians attempted to take over Kydonia – but without success. However, we do have a much more complete picture of what the city's architecture was like during the Hellenistic and, especially, the Roman periods. Excavations have uncovered various types of tombs, such as the chamber tomb and the cist grave, as well as abundant grave offerings of all sorts from figurines to gold jewelry. According to literary testimonies, Kydonia adjoined the cities of

3rd c. AD mosaic floor in the city of Chania showing Poseidon and the nymph Amymone

12

Section of a stone frieze from Chania, 7ᵗʰ c. AD.

Polichna, Pergamos and Keraia, whose positions have yet to be definitively recognized; their locations shift depending on the particular scholar's point of view. Kydonia was a rival with the other large cities of western Crete (Falassarna, Elyros, Polyrrinia, and Aptera) and was often at war with them. Polybius tells that Kydonia fought on the side of Knossos during the war between Knossos and Lyttos in 220 BC. But it fought against Knossos and Gortyn in 189 BC. However, starting in 67 BC with the occupation by the Roman consul Quinctius Metellus, Kydonia and the rest of Crete entered a period of great prosperity. Kydonia was an independent city and had its own coins that circulated in many different types. Several bear the head of either Artemis or Apollo on one side and the word KYDONIATAN on the other along with a hunting scene or Kydon being suckled by a wolf.

Coins from Kydonia

Early Christian Times
Early Byzantine Period
Arab Rule
Middle Byzantine Period

The most important early Christian finds come from Kastelli hill. The remains of an early Christian basilica have been discovered directly under the Venetian cathedral or Duomo. Elsewhere in area early Christian tombs and stray relics from the same period have been unearthed. It is certain that Kydonia was continuously inhabited until the end of the First Byzantine period given that it is cited as the see of the bishop of Kydonia in the 7ᵗʰ Ecumenical Council (of Nicaea), which took place in 787. Equally meager in archeological finds is the period of Arab rule, which began in 823 when the Saracens seized Crete and lasted until 961. It must have been during this period, and more precisely c. 828, that Kydonia was destroyed, as were most of the other cities on Crete.

The only indication we have of settlement in the Kydonia area during the Middle Byzantine period (961-1252) is the fortification wall on Kastelli hill. It is likely, moreover, that the hill took its name from this wall. During this era it appears, too, that the name Kydonia was replaced by the name Chania. The old name

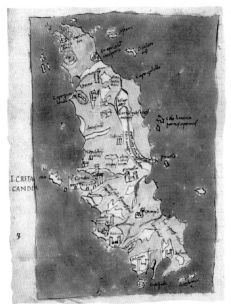

Map by Buondelmondi

continued to be used only in the bishop's title, for obvious historical reasons, although the bishopric itself probably was located at the settlement of Episkopi, Aghia community. The new name is mentioned for the first time as "Cania" in a document from 1211 and as "Canea" in 1252. Opinions vary as to the origin and etymology of the name. According to the philologist and archaeologist Stefanos Zanthoudidis, it comes from the Arabic Al-Hanim (=hani, that is inn, plural Chania). Later, the "al" was mistakenly considered to be an article and thus "translated" in the Greek as "ta" and in Latin as "la". This also explains the reference by Buondelmondi to Laghanea and the corresponding Greek name LaChanias. Another opinion has it that the name comes from a type of fish, the hanno or hanni, that is comber (plural hannia). The prevailing interpretation is the one provided by the archaeologist Nikolaos Platon. He claims that the name Chania comes from the place name AlChania hamlet, and there is also an inscription testifying to this. The place name comes from the god Velhanus or Valhanus, who was worshipped in Crete and was none other than Hephaestus (=Vulcanus). The worship of Velhanus has been verified archeologically from the discovery in Aghia Triada Heraklion of a sanctuary dedicated to the god and documented by inscriptions bearing his name. To the Arab ear AlChania sounded like Al Hanim (the hani) and, as stated above, the "Al" was later thought to be an article and translated as "ta" Chania or "la" Canea.

Section of the Byzantine wall

Venetian Rule

The period of the Venetian rule officially began in 1204 when Crete passed into the hands of Boniface of Monferrat as a result of the Fourth Crusade. Boniface then proceeded to sell it to the Venetians. However, in 1206 the Genoese pirate Enrico Pescatore, count of Malta, seized the island. Venice only managed to reclaim it in essence in 1210. The Venetian conquerors implemented a system of establishing colonies on the island to which they assigned lands appropriated from the native population. Naturally, the Cretans met this with opposition and waged a series of rebellions over the years 1211 to 1367, most of which were instigated by the local nobility. To deal with these rebellions the Venetians often implemented a system of capitulation and commensurate return, thereby ensuring the assimilation of the local nobility into the Venetian hierarchy. This is what occurred in the revolt of the "young nobles" (archontopoula) of the Skordilis and Melissinos families, which was sparked by the theft of some horses from a Venetian castellan (equal to castle governor). The revolt soon spread throughout all of western Crete, forcing the Venetians to capitulate in 1219 with the rebels securing land and other privileges. The subsequent uprising in 1222 led to a new pact in 1224. In yet another rebellion in 1228, which was also the most consequential, the leaders of the same "archontopoula" requested the aid of the emperor of Nicaea, John III Ducas Vatatzes. Vatatzes initially agreed but later backed out. The revolt ended in capitulation to the leader of the Melissinos and Demonoyannis families, who secured large tracts of land in exchange for helping the Venetians to oust Vatatzes' troops. Vatatzes' troops remained in Crete, occupying the fortress of Aghios Nikolaos in Apokoronas, Chania. Of course, this pact did not mean an end to the rebellions. Characteristic was the Drakontopoulos family's categorical refusal to submit or even negotiate, which resulted in them declaring themselves enemies of Venice. Despite the strong and constant opposition, the Venetians proceeded with a series of administrative reforms by which the island,

Map by Benedetto Bordone, 1528

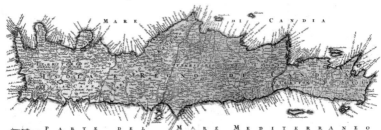

The administrative division of Crete by the Venetians

which was called a "Kingdom" (Regno di Candia) until the early 14th century, was divided into six districts (sestieri), each of which contained at least two turmae or administrative units. With this division the region of Chania formed the Sexterio of Dorsodurno, which included the turmae of Chania, Kissamos, and Selino.

Later, from the early 14th century and for the remainder of the

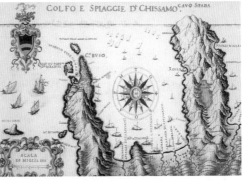

The **Territorio della Canea** (Department of Chania) included 3 castellaniae or military units: 1. **Apokoronas**, with its seat at Kastelli Apokoronas (Castel Apicorono), near what is now the village of Kalyves; 2. **Kissamos**, with its seat at Kastelli of Kissamos (Castel Chissmmo), in what is now the town of Kastelli; 3. **Selino**, with its seat at Kastelli of Selino (Castel Selino), near today's Paleohora. **Sfakia** was the one region in Chania that has never been castellania. Instead, it answered directly to Chania and maintained a semiautonomous regime since the Venetians were incapable of imposing total authority on this inaccessible region. Only in the last centuries of their rule did the Venetians manage to build two fortresses, one in the village of Sfakia and the other in Frangokastello. Drawings by Francesco Basilicata, 1618.

According to the 1630 description by the military architect Francesco Basilicata, Chania had a Byzantine fortress that contained the first majestic Venetian buildings (Duomo, Rector's residence, nobles' homes), a large central boulevard (la corsa), a fountain, an aqueduct, a fortification with five bastions that encircled the entire city and whose construction began in 1536, dockyard vaults, a breakwater, lighthouse, and churches such as San Nicolo in Splantzia, Lady of Mercy, Aghios Frangiskos, etc.

Venetian occupation, Crete was divided into four departments or territorii (di Candia, di Rettimo, della Canea,

Relief carving with the Venetian lion in Chania (Pashley)

di Sitia) with their corresponding capitals Handaka, Rethymnon, Chania, and Sitia. The highest authority on the island was held by the Duke (Duca), whose seat was in Handaka, with the aid of two Advisors (Consiglieri). Each of the provinces of Chania, Rethymnon, and Sitia was governed by a Rector (Rettore) who had political and military duties. Sfakia, on the other hand, had a Lookout (proveditore). The military command of the entire island was the responsibility of the Captain (capitan general) and the lesser ranking castellans, namely the governors of the local castellaniae or military units. With the fall of Constantinople in 1453 Venice's position in the East began to deteriorate.

The Turkish threat steadily increased as of the early 16th century. In 1527 Turkish pirates looted two ships in the Chania area, and in 1538 the famous pirate Khayr ad-Din Barbarossa (Redbeard) set out from Chania to plunder the entire island. In 1539 he

Barbarossa or Redbeard

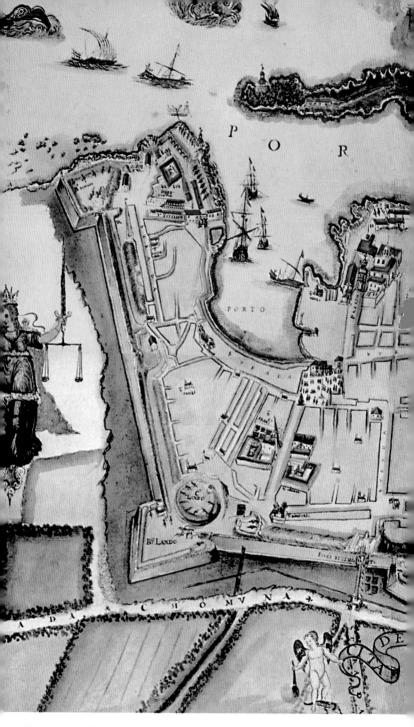

The Venetians colonized Chania in 1252. They gave it the name La Canea and settled on Kastelli hill where a Byzantine wall already existed. There they built the Duomo della Santa Maria, the rector's residence and several other officers' residences. A settlement (the "burgo") grew up along the slopes of the hill outside the castle and was later

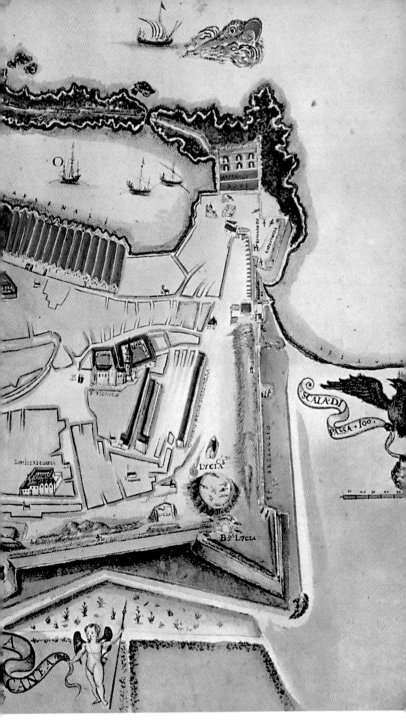

enclosed by a new wall. This was also the pattern in the other departments of Crete.
There is no confirming excavation evidence, however, of testimony of a wall surrounding
the burgo during the 14th century. Drawing by G. Corner, 1652.

Pirate galleon from Barbary

overtook the fortress of Selino. In 1571 the Turks landed at the port of Suda, plundered all the surrounding villages, and took captive hordes of inhabitants.

The Turkish threat on the one hand and the Venetian coexistence with the Cretans on the other despite the revolts of the previous centuries resulted in the Cretans and Venetians developing a harmonious relationship with one another, with little conflict. The native Cretans not only actively participated in Venetian naval operations against the Turks but also backed them financially. With all these efforts Venice managed to secure both its rule of the island as well as the collaboration of the

A stroll through the old town of Chania is enough to convince any visitor that the city's public buildings were designed with architectural innovations identical to those in the Metropolis, Venice.

Cretans. At the same time, in 1536 Venice commissioned the Veronese architect Michele Sanmicheli

Drawing by Coronelli, 1696.

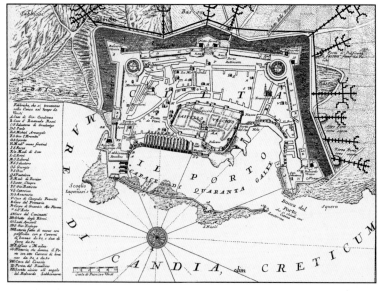

to design the new fortifications of Chania, to be completed by the end of the 16th century. In addition, the region's fortress was bolstered by defense works on the islets of Aghii Theodori and Aghios Nikolaos in Suda Bay and in Gramvoussa at the northwestern tip of Crete.

The Cretan-Venetian coexistence created economic and artistic conditions favorable to the development of a local culture, which came to be known as the "Cretan Renaissance." Local tradition gradually assimilated Venetian culture during the 16th and 17th centuries, the last two centuries of Venetian rule. The Venetians adopted the Cretan lifestyle and the Cretans assimilated western influences in the fields of art, literature and architecture.

The Siege

Despite the normalization of relations between the Cretans and Venetians and even with the ramparts funded by the Doge to bolster the island's defenses, the Turks never gave up the prospect of conquering the island that would give them a strategic superiority in the Mediterranean. An insignificant incident provided them with the opportunity when, in 1644, pirate Hospitalers captured a ship off the coast of Rhodes filled with pilgrims on their way to Mecca. They landed briefly

in Crete before sailing for their own island of Malta. The Turks were outraged and accused the Venetians of violating their treaties and collaborating with the pirates.

The Turks embarked on a surprise invasion of Crete in 1645 after

Turkish shells at Gonia Monastery

first misleading the Venetians into believing that they were planning to attack Malta. They reached the western coast of the Gulf of Chania on 22 June and landed on the shores of Gonia, east of the

Merian, Theatri Europaei, Frankfurt, 1651

IL CASTELO DI S. TODARO RAQVISTATO

Aghii Theodori

Spatha promontory. From there they easily ravaged the Monastery of Odigitria and began moving eastward by land and by sea towards the city of Chania. The fleet's next stop was the islet of Aghii Theodori, where there were two forts. One was derelict, the other had 70 soldiers and a few canons. When Commander Giuliani refused to surrender, the Turks surrounded Thodorou on 24 June and disembarked on her unprotected side. Giuliani raised the

Surda (O. Danner)

white flag in an attempt at negotiation. But when faced with the Turks' indifference to his offer, he set fire to the ammunition, blowing up the fort and all the Turks and Christians inside it.

While this was happening at sea, the Turkish army was proceeding by land, pillaging village after village and reaching the outskirts of Chania. On 27 June 1645 the Turkish army and 80 galleons landed

Venetian Galleon

in city and began its siege. Fifty days later, on 22 August 1645, Chania surrendered to the Turks with some favorable terms. These included allowing those inhabitants who wished to, to leave the city or to remain with the enjoyment of certain privileges.

While all this was going on 15 galleons under the command of Antonio Marino Capello had anchored in Suda Bay, in May 1645, to safeguard the port. But when the Turkish fleet began moving towards Suda, Capello deserted his fleet for no apparent reason. After many unsuccessful

The siege of Chandakas (Herakleion) began in 1648 and lasted 21 years before the city fell into the hands of the conquerors. The surrender of all Crete (except for Suda, which remained Venetian until 1715, Gramvoussa until 1692, and Spinalonga) was signed on 16 September 1669. In addition to the demographic and economic decline of the island, the siege of Crete and its being assigned as an Ottoman dominion also meant the deterioration of the "Cretan Renaissance" in terms of art and culture.

The siege of Chania. Merian, Theatri Europaei, Frankfurt, 1651

SCOGLIO ET FORTEZZA DELLA SVDA

The fortress of
Aghios Nikolaos at
Suda, 17th c.

◀ Fr. Basilicata,
1618

O. Dapper, 1703
▼

attempts by land as well the fleet's new commander, Giovani Capello, reached Suda in June 1646, bringing with him 27 galleons with munitions. The strategic positions around Suda, Kalami, Malaxa, and the fortress of Apokoronas itself were unable to restrain the Turkish movement toward Rethymnon. At the same time, while naval forces still held the fortress of Suda - actually the fortified islet at the entrance to the port - the Venetian infantry began moving westward to reinforce those regions. Sometime in August the siege of the fort of Suda began. But even though it suffered numerous devastations, it never fell into Turkish hands mainly because of island's steep drop into the sea and the ramparts that the Venetians constructed. It was only in 1715, long after all Crete had surrendered, that Suda finally surrendered too.

Ottoman Rule

The siege of Chania and the subsequent conquest of all Crete by the Turks put a halt to the creative advances of the Cretan renaissance. The cultural impact notwithstanding, there were also population losses and an overall economic decline. Naturally, Venice did not want to believe that it had lost Crete even after the signed surrender of 1669. It continued to fight for and managed to hold on to the fortresses of Gramvoussa, Suda and Spinalonga, believing that they could be used as bases in a subsequent attempt to retake the island. Indeed, they made their first attempt to recapture Chania in 1692, and the Venetians sent Domenico Mocenigo to take possession of it. Despite the forty-day standoff and their strong ground reinforcements, Mocenigo was forced to retreat. The sad toll of this effort was the destruction of Apokoronas and Sfakia. The Venetians finally lost the fortress of Gramvoussa in 1691 and Suda in 1715 in

The Rethymnian Valide Sultana Evmenia Vergitsi

Venetian lion in Gramvoussa

the Venetian-Turkish wars. The new conquerors created the **"Eyâlet of Crete"**, that is a supreme administrative unit of the Ottoman empire, which initially divided Crete into four sections along the Venetian lines (Sitia, Handaka, Rethymnon, Chania). They later merged Sitia with Handaka to create three. Sfakia alone maintained a peculiar form of independence

Map of Crete with Ottoman symbols

that was initially attributed to their being assigned to the protection of the sultan's mother (valide). Handakas was the capital of the eyâlet, and a pasha appointed by the sultan governed each department. According to the French traveler Pitton de Tournefort, 2000 Cretans and 1500 Turks were living in Chania at the end of the 17th century, figures that indicate the distillation of the native population. The population noticeably increased during the 18th century when the ratio of Greeks to Turks on the entire island was estimated at 200,000 to 150,000.

Besides the changes at

Cretan man c. 18th century

every level, the most significant impact of Turkish occupation was on the island's intellectual life. The Cretan scholars of prior years had scattered to other parts of Greece and abroad, and the island fell into virtual darkness. One shining exception, however, was the activity of certain monasteries and monks. The Gonia Monastery in the Chania area, which had an important library, became a major center for manuscript copying and Bishop Arsenios of Kydonia a distinguished figure in letters.

Only towards the end of the 18th century would an attempt be made at educational reform, and we have testimony that there were two schools operating in Chania in 1791. We also have testimony from the early 19th century of the presence of scholars who had undertaken the job of education

Chania from the east (O. Dapper, 1703)

CANEA.

Turkish fountain in the harbor

central mosque (Hünkar Camii). The pasha now lived in the stately home on Kastelli hill that once housed the rector of Chania. The city was embellished with mosques, baths

Splantzia Square with the "Arabian pavilion" and the church of St Nicholas as a Mosque.

and who cultivated the revolutionary spirit. Immediately after their victory, the Turks did what they could to alter the city's appearance and demonstrate their domination in every way. One of their first projects was to convert the Venetian cathedrals and monasteries into mosques. In Splantzia, a neighborhood that they had chosen along with Kastelli to settle in en masse, they turned the Dominican Cathedral of St. Nicholas into the

and fountains, buildings directly associated with Muslim religious and cultural customs. Revolutionary activities were initiated in Sfakia in April 1821. Conditions on the island were extremely difficult because the Greeks lacked weapons

and primarily because the Turks greatly outnumbered them. The Turks retaliated to the first victorious battle on 14 June 1821 with revenge attacks and hangings. Among the victims was the Bishop of Kissamos Melchizedek

Chania Harbor (Illustrated London News)

Clashes between Cretans and Turks on the streets of Chania (Petit Parisien)

ended ingloriously. The European forces intervened in 1830 and it was decided that Crete should remain under the jurisdiction of the sultan and outside the boundaries of the newly formed Greek state. The sultan, in turn, granted it to Mehmet Ali of Egypt in reward for his aid in squelching the Cretan revolt. Crete remained under Egyptian occupation until 1841. In efforts to construct a series of public works, the Egyptians levied heavy taxes. This provoked Cretan opposition. One of the most significant insurrections, which came to be known as the "Mournia movement" after the region of the same name in Kydonia, started in September 1833. This movement made clear to the Great Powers the people's dissatisfaction with

Mehmet Ali

Despotakis, who was hanged in the Splantzia central square, along with all the monks of the Monastery of Prodromos in Akrotiri. Despite the victorious battles throughout western Crete during the summer of 1821, in August the Turks arrived in Sfakia and destroyed it. The Cretans, however, did not cease their rebellious activity, so Sultan Mahmut asked Mehmet Ali of Egypt for assistance. Mehmet sent his powerful forces to the island in 1822. By 1824, after dozens of skirmishes, the Egyptians had squelched the Cretan revolt. A new effort – successful this time – in 1825 secured the occupation of the fortresses of Gramvoussa and Kissamos, rekindling the Cretan insurgence in the Chania region, which later spread throughout Crete. Still, the many years of struggle

Cretan revolutionaries

Egypt's economic measures as well as with the political and military authorities. The Great Powers ignored the protest and the Egyptian authorities retaliated with attacks and hangings. Once again, the inhabitants of the Chania region began their revolutionary efforts with heavy fighting in Vrysses and Vafe of Apokoronas. But to no avail. In the end Crete remained under Egyptian occupation until 1841 when it was returned to the sultan. In 1851 the capital of the eyâlet of Crete was moved from Handaka to Chania. The most important development in the years to follow was the adoption in 1856 of the **Hatt i Hümayun**, by which the sultan gave Christians the rights of religious freedom, property ownership and personal freedom. The Turks,

Cretan peasants and Chania from Halepa (Edward Lear, 1864)

however, did their best to limit these rights. Ten years of constant violations of the Hatt i Hümayun led to the great Cretan uprising, which began in 1866 and lasted until 1869. Ioannis Zymbrakakis was appointed military leader for the Chania area. Next came the heroic insurgence in Arkadi, followed by of the 1869 uprising, and in 1877 yet another revolutionary movement began in Chania. In 1878 a treaty was signed in Halepa that secured numerous privileges for Christians and stipulated that the Governor General of Crete could be Christian. Nevertheless, internal conflicts and the emergence of rival

Chania destroyed by fire in January 1897

The annihilation in Arkadi in 1866 served to kindle European awareness and accelerated the process of Enosis or union with the rest of Greece.

skirmishes in eastern Crete. The situation in Crete became desperate after the suppression parties created major problems. Apathy and anarchy among the revolutionaries resulted in the totally fruitless five-year period between 1890 and 1895. At last, on 18 July 1898, the Great Powers intervened and the autonomous **"Cretan State"** was founded with Prince George of Greece as high commissioner. By the end of November of the same year, the Turkish army had completed its final withdrawal from the island.

Vessels of the Great Powers outside Chania Harbor (Illustrated London News)

Autonomy

During the period of autonomy, Crete was under the protection of the European forces and under the sultan's high suzerainty. The constitution that was passed in 1899 gave it the institutional status of State with Prince George, the son of the Greek king, as High Commissioner

Prince George

and deputy of the Great Powers. These conditions made Crete a state with a semi-autonomous regime. The Cretans considered this status transitional and the High Commissioner himself promoted the island's union with the rest of Greece. The protecting forces, however, did

not share the same opinion, given that they associated Crete with their own interests. The diplomatic efforts of the Greek state and Prince George proved fruitless, except for certain concessions that granted aid to a local army and the recognition of the Cretan flag. Moreover, the unfortunate outcome of the Prince's efforts combined with his conflict from the outset with Justice Advisor Eleftherios Venizelos made him generally unpopular with the Cretans. Eleftherios Venizelos maintained that union with Greece had to be a gradual process, the first stage of which was the finalization of autonomy. This view differed from George's, who advocated the "Great Island's" immediate union with

Eleftherios Venizelos

the Kingdom of Greece. Adhering strictly to the political trends of the west, Venizelos introduced the concept of liberalism with a movement strongly influenced by the principles of the French revolutionaries. Fundamental to his program were the protection of the rights of man, the orderly functioning of the state, and the economic recovery of the land. His leadership was responsible for organizing the

Delegates of the Great Powers receiving Prince George

Rebel headquarters in Theriso, 1905

Alexander Zaimis, who implemented the parliamentary system with the new constitution of 1907, replaced Prince George. In July of 1908 the foreign military forces began leaving the island, with a view to completing their withdrawal within the following year. Negotiations and problems arising during following year

opposition faction to the Prince, whose protests had reached extreme heights. In March 1905 a revolt broke out in the village of Theriso-Chania demanding union with Greece and the immediate resignation of the High Commissioner. The protecting powers proved to be totally inadequate in quelling the armed action, so Venizelos requested a special delegation of representatives of the Powers to investigate the matter. In its findings submitted in March 1906, the

International Investigating Committee stated that Crete must be formally united with

Alexander Zaimis landing in Chania

the Kingdom of Greece as quickly as possible. Shortly afterwards, in September,

created a setback to a permanent solution to the Cretan issue, making it necessary for

The Municipal Market of Chania

Venizelos to leave Crete and move to Athens. Even though the Cretan parliamentarians were admitted into the Greek parliament in October 1912, official union was not self-evident. Crete remained an autonomous regime, but only formally. On 14 February 1913 the flag of the Great Powers was lowered on the fort of Suda and in November the King of the Greeks arrived in Crete. At last, the Greek flag was raised on the Firkas in the old city of Chania.

In the years that followed, the event most strongly affecting Chania was the German bombardment of 1941, which truly struck at the heart of the old city, Kastelli. Some decisions made on demolition of several public and private buildings and implemented during German occupation were disastrous. Fortunately, Chania was declared a historical monument in 1965, preserving all that

The Greek flag flies on the Firkas

survived for Chania to remain the jewel of

During the period of autonomy the size and face of the city of Chania altered significantly. Suburbs were built, such as Halepa, the principal aristocratic quarter with its grand neoclassical mansions that housed the envoys of the Great Powers. Neoclassicism was the prevailing style in urban dwellings as well public buildings.

During the same period, the wooden enclosed balconies added by the Turks to the facades of Venetian houses were dismantled. Unfortunately, many sections of the Venetian fortifications were also demolished at this time to create roads and expand the city beyond the old walls. The famous Municipal Market of Chania is built on top of sections of the old moat.

MONUMENTS

Fortifications

The Byzantine Wall

The Byzantine wall surrounded the first settlement hub of Chania, the hill of Kastelli. Parts of the foundations of the city's earlier Hellenistic wall have been found in its foundations. The Venetians, who gave this area the name castel vecchio, would proceed to make it their residence and seat, altering and augmenting the already existing wall. Today fragments of the Byzantine wall survive only in certain spots around the city due to the fact that most of it was buried when the city was rebuilt. Still, the existing portions provide enough information for us to recreate an image of how it once looked. The wall that surrounded the naturally fortified hill had defense works mainly on the south side and to some extent on the east and west. It followed an irregular line and had small rectangular or polygonal towers and four gates: two main gates on the east and west sides, and two secondary gates on the south and north. Practically nothing survives of these gates today. Their positions have been determined at the following points: the east gate at the intersection of Kanevaro and Daskaloyanni Streets; the west gate in Sintrivaniou Square; the north gate on Afentouliev Street; and the south gate at the junction of Katre and Karaoli Dimitriou Streets.

A large tower, of which nothing survives today, protected the west gate that was located at the west end of Kanevaro

Building material from ancient Kydonia was used to construct the wall. As a result, ancient architectural fragments are visible in many places where the wall is preserved, such as on Karaoli Dimitriou and Sifaka Streets.

Street. A neoclassical house now stands in its place. There must have been a similar tower at the east gate, too, where Kanevaro Street joins Daskaloyanni. A tower also stood in what is now Katehaki Square, on the north side of the wall. Portions of it survive under the existing houses. This section of the wall was used during the construction of the Venetian monastery of Santa Maria dei Miracoli.

The Kastelli

As we've seen, the naturally fortified hill of Kastelli was the primary settlement site in Chania since ancient times. There is proof of the existence of a Hellenistic wall encircling it, as well as a later Byzantine wall. It was inevitable that the Venetian colonizers arriving in Chania in 1252 would make use of the already fortified hill, which they called **castel vecchio.** There, they constructed their cathedral, palaces and stately homes. Thus fortified, Kastelli became the city center. According to a report made by Basilicata in 1630, the central square of Kastelli contained a beautiful fountain whose water came by aqueduct from three miles away. The settlement's main street was the Corso, and is today's Kanevaro Street. The Corso ran east to west, connecting the castle's two main gates and dividing the city into two sections, north and south. Maps from this time tell us that a Palazzo stood at the northwest end of

The Rector's home

which survives to this day. In addition to the Palazzo, in Kastelli there were luxurious private homes for the nobility such as the Premarin and the Giancarolo mansions, as well as the cathedral or Duomo of Santa Maria. Bombs in World War II destroyed the castle's central gates.

town (at the north end of today's Lithinon Street). Remains of its first and second floors still exist. The Turkish Government House was then built on this same spot in 1845, two centuries later. It too was demolished to build the new Government House,

Doorframes of private homes in Kastelli

The New Walls

According to Basilicata's descriptions and reports, the Byzantine fortification surrounded the old city along with the rector's residence, the mansions of the nobles and the cathedral. The "burgo" or new town gradually

grew up outside the walls so the Venetians needed to create new walls.

The **Porta Retimiota** (Gate of Rethymnon),

the main gate of the new wall, stood on its south side, near the city's modern covered market. Another gate, the **Porta Sabbionara**

Sabbionara bastion

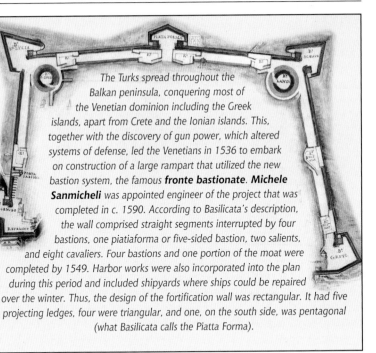

The Turks spread throughout the Balkan peninsula, conquering most of the Venetian dominion including the Greek islands, apart from Crete and the Ionian islands. This, together with the discovery of gun power, which altered systems of defense, led the Venetians in 1536 to embark on construction of a large rampart that utilized the new bastion system, the famous **fronte bastionate**. **Michele Sanmicheli** was appointed engineer of the project that was completed in c. 1590. According to Basilicata's description, the wall comprised straight segments interrupted by four bastions, one piatiaforma or five-sided bastion, two salients, and eight cavaliers. Four bastions and one portion of the moat were completed by 1549. Harbor works were also incorporated into the plan during this period and included shipyards where ships could be repaired over the winter. Thus, the design of the fortification wall was rectangular. It had five projecting ledges, four were triangular, and one, on the south side, was pentagonal (what Basilicata calls the Piatta Forma).

(Gate of the Sands) stood on the northeast end of town and led to the shore. Lastly, on the southeast was the **gate of San Salvatore**, near the bastion of the same name.

The Firkas fortress stands to the west of the harbor and was built to protect it.

Firkas is Turkish for barracks. It served as headquarters for the commanding officer and contained military facilities and munitions depots. West of the Firkas was the **bastion of San Salvatore**, which contained the monastery of the same name and the service postern gate to the fortification enclosure. The square vaulted building in the place currently housing the antiquities conservation workshop was an ammunition depot. Above the bastion of San Salvatore, which is sometimes called Griti or Venier, is the salient of the same name, built

Gunpowder Depot

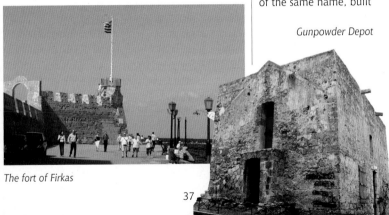

The fort of Firkas

Kum Kapi

to further reinforce the defense of the harbor and the western section of the fortress. The west wing of the battlement follows a straight line interrupted only at its midpoint by the **salient of Priuli.** Shortly before the wall's southwest corner is the circular **salient of Lando.** The wall then turns east to form its south wing, in the middle of which stood the large **Piatta Forma bastion**. The primary purpose of this defense tower, on top of which was built the covered municipal market of today, was

to protect the fortress's main gate, the Porta Retimiotta, as well as the entire south wing of the ramparts. This gate, which the Turks would call Kale-Kapi (Gate to the Fortress), was so named because it faced Rethymnon. The ramparts continue beyond Piatta Forma and end at the bastion of **Santa Lucia** and the salient of the same name, which form the southeast tip of the fortress. At

this point the wall turns north and ends at Porta Sabbionara or Kum Kapi, as the Turks called it, meaning Gate of the Sands.

To the north of this gate is the **bastion of Sabbionara or Mocenigo**, whose façade has a relief carving of the lion of Saint Mark. The rocky segment running northward, which Basilicata calls Lagonisi, forms the jetty that terminates the wall to the west and creates the harbor. There is another small gate on the north side of the ramparts, called "Portaki" or little door, which was used exclusively for military purposes.

In addition to the main and service gates, the wall also had two arches, one at the northwest edge of the town and one northeast.

*Nothing survives of the majestic **Porta Retimiota**, with its three arched openings and equal number of spires. It was demolished in 1911. We know what it looked like thanks to Corner's 1625 drawing and to G. Gerola's photographs and drawings.*

Circular Lando cavalier

The northwest arch, called **Porta Kolombo**, had contained a sculpture of the winged

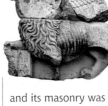

lion of Venice holding the Gospels with the inscription "AVE MARCE EUAGELISTA MEUS". The arch was demolished in 1918 and the sculpture was removed to the archeological museum. The northeast arch was demolished in 1916

and its masonry was used to construct the schoolyard entrance on Daskaloyanni Street. The new Venetian ramparts were positioned around the old Kastelli fortress in such a way as to provide enough room within the walls to create four elegant town squares - Splantzia, Syntrivani (= fountain), and Aghii Anargyri - and

the main Katolas gate. The Venetians used these squares mostly for waterworks. Splantzia Square contained an aqueduct dating from this era, which was maintained until 1856. A majestic marble fountain graced the center of Syntrivani Square. The Venetians also opened a well in Aghii Anargyri Square, which was maintained until 1915.

The Harbor & Shipyards

From the start, the lack of a natural harbor created problems for the city of Chania. There are records from as early as the 14th century of attempts to carry out harbor works. But the powerful northerly winds and the relentless sand incursions on the eastern side of the harbor buffeted these efforts. The boulders along the northern coast favored the construction of a jetty that was reinforced by a wall in 1515. The **bastion of Aghios Nikolaos** was built in the center of the harbor, named after the little church

The large complex with its 17 shipyards was completed in 1599, whereas construction of the complex of five shipyards known as the Moro shipyards and located between the jetty and the Sabbionara bastion, began in 1607. Today only two shipyards survive from the small complex and eight from the large one. Of these, seven are adjoining. The eighth, further south, had a second story added to it at later date and was used as the Christian Community schoolhouse. The Chania customs house was erected on the site of the demolished Venetian structures. These earlier structures were long and narrow with vaulted roofs terminating in pediments. The narrow end faced north, opening directly on to the sea to facilitate hauling the ships onto dry land. The south end contained the entrance to the shipyards along with the skylights and windows to provide light. The façade of the buildings was walled up sometime later.

inside it dedicated to that Saint. All penal executions were carried out in this bastion. Of the lighthouse on the western tip of the jetty, built during the time of Venetian rule, only the foundation remains. The lighthouse we see

today is a work from the period of Egyptian occupation and must have been constructed between 1830 and 1840.

Ships were removed to the **shipyards or Arsenal**i for repair and maintenance during the winter.

Roman Catholic Churches & Monasteries

According to Gerola's testimony, in the 17th century Chania had six monasteries, a cathedral and eight churches, of which we know only San Salvatore, the Madonna dei Renier, and San Rocco.

The Duomo

The Venetian Duomo, the cathedral of Our Lady, was located on Kastelli Hill, inside the castel vecchio where the Venetians had settled.

Remains of the Duomo along with those of the earlier buildings underneath it are visible in the Square of Aghia Katerini and on Kanevaro Street. According to Gerola, the bishopric of Aghia, which had moved to Chania by 1400, was also located here. Recent excavations have revealed the foundations of an early Christian basilica underneath the Duomo, which may have been the bishopric of Kydonia during the Early Byzantine period. This means that sometime during the Second Venetian period the bishopric of Chania (after it moved

to Aghia) returned to the same location that once held the early Christian bishopric of Kydonia. Under Turkish rule the Duomo was converted into a mosque, called Musa Pasha, and underwent many alterations to its

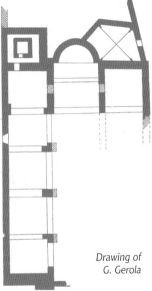

Drawing of G. Gerola

The Duomo is depicted in 16th and 17th illustrations although renderings of it vary from drawing to drawing. According to Gerola, the illustration by Coronelli from 1689, showing the lighthouse, shipyards and the Duomo, is a complete fantasy. Corner's drawing (1625) of the Duomo and the Monastery of Santa Maria dei Miracoli, on the other hand, is thought to be accurate.

architectural form. A minaret was erected on its north side in place of the campanile.
The mosque was destroyed in the German bombardment of 1941 and was later leveled entirely.

In addition to valuable photographs, Gerola also provides us with detailed descriptions. The Duomo comprised a long aisle with a vaulted chapel at each of its four far corners. The chapels were connected to the main aisle by pointed arches.

The Church of San Rocco

The Church of San Rocco, located in Splantzia Square, was probably completed in 1630. San Rocco, to whom the church is dedicated, offered protection against the Plague, and it's likely that there was an epidemic in Chania at the time of its construction.
It has an east-west orientation with its main façade on the west. It is a single-aisle, vaulted church with an aisle added along its north face that was used as a chapel or vestry. Of special note are its west and south sides. The main façade on the west has an impressive portal with a lintel and rose window, and terminates in pediment.
The south side contains a pedimental lintel over its main portal and two large windows. Running the entire length of the architrave on the south side is the inscription DEO O.M. ET D. ROCCO DICATVM.M.D.CXXX ("dedicated to the most good and greatest God and Holy Rocco. 1630"). During the period of Turkish rule, the church was converted into a military guardhouse.

The Madonna dei Renier

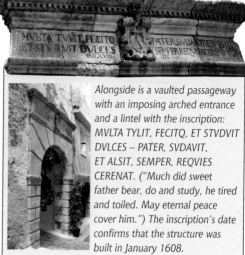

Alongside is a vaulted passageway with an imposing arched entrance and a lintel with the inscription: MVLTA TYLIT, FECITQ, ET STVDVIT DVLCES – PATER, SVDAVIT, ET ALSIT, SEMPER, REQVIES CERENAT. ("Much did sweet father bear, do and study, he tired and toiled. May eternal peace cover him.") The inscription's date confirms that the structure was built in January 1608.

This little church of Our Lady got its name from the family in whose palace it was built. In other words, it was the chapel of the palace located at the small lane off Theofanous Street. The structure is vaulted and rectangular with a rose window on its west wall and a portal with a late Gothic lintel at the drum of which are traces of fresco.

The Monastery of Aghios Frangiskos (St. Francis)

This, the largest Roman Catholic Church in Chania is located on today's Halidon Street. Under Turkish rule it was converted into a mosque. It was renamed Yusuf Pasha mosque and acquired a minaret on its northwest corner,

The katholikon comprised a church with three chapels on the east that communicate with each other and the central nave by way of arched openings, as we see in Gerola's photograph. There are aisles to the north and south of the central nave that communicate by way of semicircular arches. The vault rests on arches.

remains of which still exist. We don't know for certain when the church was erected. But it must have existed in 1595 because a letter written by Onorio Belli in 1596 reports not only the existence of the church but also that its steeple listed in an earthquake. According to Venetian period maps and drawings, the complex comprised a church with a tall bell

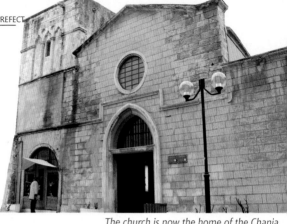

The church is now the home of the Chania Archeological Museum.

tower on its east side, a group of monks' cells on the south, and a garden on the north. A row of three chapels with groined roofs was later added to the north side. The westernmost part of the church, which also contains the minaret, has two aisles and is an annex built under Turkish rule.

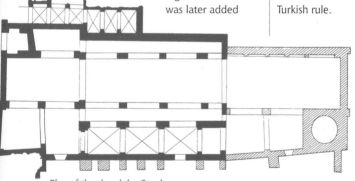

Plan of the church by Gerola

The Convent of Santa Chiara

According to drawings, maps, and documents of the day, the Convent of Santa Chiara was located directly opposite the Monastery of St. Francis, across Ruga Magistra (today's Halidon Street). This convent belonged to the sisters of the Franciscan order and must have been built in the early 15th century by order of Pope Boniface IX to the Bishop of Aghia. A bathhouse was built in its place during the Turkish occupation, which still survives.

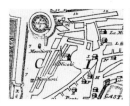

The Monastery of Aghios Nikolaos (Saint Nicolas)

The Church of Aghios Nikolaos in Splantzia Square was also the katholikon or main church of the Dominican monastery of the same name in the Chania region. Written testimony informs us that it must have been built around 1320. According to maps and drawings of the day, it contained a katholikon or central nave with a steeple and two vaulted porticos on its north side. The bell tower and a large portion of the porticos no longer survive.

The church was a single-aisle basilica with a wooden, Λ-shaped roof and an east-west orientation. The wooden roof was replaced in modern times by a cement roof. The central portion of its three-part east section was groin-vaulted.

During Turkish occupation the church was converted into a mosque. It was renamed Hünkar Camii and acquired a minaret with two balconies on the southwest corner of its façade.

In 1919 it acquired an apse in the eastern end and since then has operated as the Greek Orthodox Church of Aghios Nikolaos.

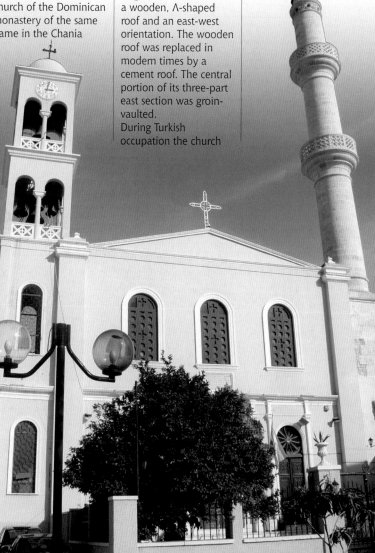

The Monastery of San Salvatore

This small monastery on the northwestern end of the fortified town belonged to the Franciscan brothers. Under Turkish occupation the church was converted into a mosque and renamed Topu Han or Topana. The church has a single aisle and a vaulted roof with no bell tower. On its north side there are two chapels with groin vaults, which communicate with central nave by archways. The north wall of the central nave contains an apse decorated with carved columns and anthemia, that is honeysuckle ornament. The floor of this space also contains tombs.

The Convent of Santa Maria dei Miracoli

The convent of Our Lady of the Miracles belonged to the Dominican sisters and was built inside Kastelli hill, more or less opposite the Duomo. According to an inscription, the church was built in 1606 by Marussa Mengano. But Corner's drawing, dated 1625, shows us that the monastery with its single-aisle katholikon also had a bell tower, a courtyard and a row of cells on the south side of the katholikon. Surviving today is the south wall of the church, sections of the east wall, and a small portion of the cells.

The Convent of Santa Maria de la Misericordia

This convent, dedicated to Our Lady of Mercy, belonged to the nuns of the Augustinian order. It was then used by the Turks as a residence. What little is left of the convent may be seen on Hadji Michali Daliani Street.

A decree was handed down based on the sisters' request to rebuild the convent after it was demolished during the fortification of the city.

Drawings from that period tell us that the convent had a nearly square plan and contained a courtyard. The larger portion of the south side was taken up by the façade of the katholikon. The other three sides held the nuns' cells and other auxiliary spaces. Today all that survives of the complex are portions of the west and north wings.

Greek Orthodox Churches

Aghia Ekaterini (Saint Katherine)

In Splantzia Square, close to Aghios Nikolaos, one also finds the two-aisle basilica dedicated to Saint Katherine and Saint John the Hermit. In the center of its façade, where the two aisles can be clearly discerned, there is a bi-lobed belfry, of which only the base is preserved. Over the stone portals with their ornamented lintels are relieving semicircular niches that are supported by piers. Above these are rose windows. The basilica dates from the second half of the 16th century.

The Trimartyri

If you walk downhill on Halidon Street you will come to a large square, or plateia, on your right, which is dominated by the metropolitan cathedral of Chania. The church is also called Trimartyri because it contains three aisles. The central nave is dedicated to the Presentation of the Virgin, the north aisle to Aghios Nikolaos (St. Nicholas), and the south aisle to the three Great Church Fathers, i.e. St. Basil the Great, St. John the Chrysostom and St. Gregory of Nazianzus.

The church appears on

maps from the Venetian period, so we know that it existed at that time. During Turkish rule it was converted into a soap factory, owned by Mustafa Pasha Naili or Giritli. Tradition has it that, thanks to the good intentions of Mustafa Pasha, the icon of the Virgin from the former church remained in the soap factory and its lamp kept lit. The icon was later taken to the Monastery of Aghia Triada (Holy Trinity) of Giancarolo. In the mid-1800s, the soap-maker Tserkakis saw a vision of the Virgin Mary who told him that her domicile must cease to be used as a soap factory. Later, when Mustafa's son fell down the well, he pleaded with the Virgin to save him. The boy was indeed saved and Mustafa bequeathed the soap factory to the Christian Community together with a substantial sum of money to erect a new church that was completed in 1860. This church took over as the metropolitan cathedral of Chania, which until that time was housed in the small church of Aghii Anargyri in Splantzia Square. The cathedral was renovated in 1897 with funding from Czar Nicholas, who also donated the bell. The Trimartyri is a three-aisle basilica with a high central nave and a bell-tower at its northwest corner. Of special note in the interior is the iconostasis or altar screen with its excellent icons and the frescos that, while based on the principles of the Cretan School, are imbued with an innovative spirit and are painted with a freer hand.

Turkish Buildings

In addition to converting the Venetian churches and monasteries into mosques, the Turks also erected new monuments such as mosques, purifying baths or hamam, and fountains. Two mosques were constructed within the city and four outside it. After additions and alterations the Venetian cathedral of Aghios Nikolaos in Splantzia became the **Hünkar Camii** (the Sovereign's Mosque), the most important in the city. Its minaret had two balconies and the mosque itself was associated with a tradition whereby the sword of the Dervish who first entered it was kept in the shrine. It remained there until 1919. The Turkish residents of Chania believed that the sword possessed healing qualities.

Most impressive is the mosque of **Kuchuk Hassan** that stands intact to this day

Gazi Hussein Pasha mosque

alongside the harbor. The mosque has a grand dome, supported externally on four stone arches, and also had a minaret that was demolished in 1920. Its north and west sides contain porticoes, each topped by four smaller domes. The porticoes were originally open but later were enclosed by a wall. Each side then acquired four archways. The second mosque to be built inside the city was the **Gazi Hussein Pasha**, located near Porta Retimiota on today's Mousouron Street. In addition to these shrines and the wooden enclosed

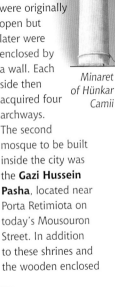

Minaret of Hünkar Camii

Kuchuk Hassan mosque

balconies that the Turks built as additions to their homes, they also embellished the city with public and private hamam and fountains. Three hamam survive in the old city: one on **Halidon Street**, one on Katre Street, and one on Zambeliou Street. The Halidon Street hamam with its multiple domes is found on the right-hand side going down

Hamam on Katre Street

towards the harbor. The hamam on **Katre Street** has a central dome encircled by smaller ones, and the **hamam on Zambeliou Street** has six domes.

Of the **fountains**, worthy of note is the octagonal fountain with the pointed cap in the courtyard of the church of Aghios Frangiskos (subsequently the Yusuf Pasha mosque and currently the Archeological Museum) on Halidon Street. Each side is decorated with fine carved reliefs that remind of a door opening with

columns, capitals, cornice, and pointed lintel. A similarly octagonal pyramidal cap resembling the upper portion of a minaret tops this octagonal structure.

Also noteworthy is the fountain on the west side of the Kuchuk Hassan Mosque, which has a simple shell shape and was built in 1880. Close by, in one of the storefronts along the harbor road is an impressive stone staircase beneath which is a lovely fountain with elaborate sculpted ornamentation. Many other fountains exist in private buildings around town.

The Turks made yet another intervention in the city

infrastructure: the **calderimi**, the cobbled roads paved with large irregular stones culled from the sea. In addition, just outside the city walls, to the south of the main gate to the ramparts, there was a Moslem **cemetery** filled with carved gravestones.

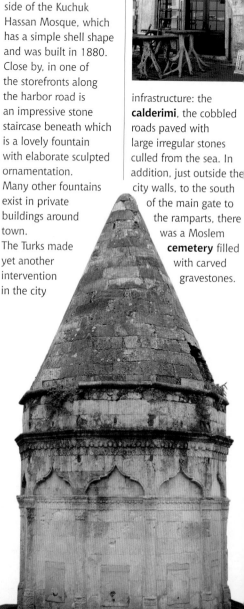

Fountain in the courtyard of Aghios Frangiskos

MUSEUMS

The Archeological Museum

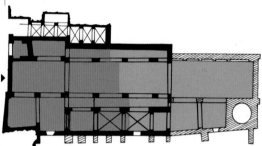

The Archeological Museum of Chania is located on Halidon Street in the Venetian church of Aghios Frangiskos that was once part of the Franciscan Monastery of the same name. During the years of Turkish rule the church was converted into the Mosque of Yusuf Pasha. In the early 20th century it was turned into movie theater called the Idaion Andron, then into a military depot, and finally, in 1962, into the Archeological Museum. The museum's exhibits trace the history of the city and prefecture from the Neolithic age to Roman times. The method of display conceptually divides the basilica into two sections: the east or fore section displaying objects from prehistoric and Minoan times, and the west or rear section where one can admire the collections from historical times.

The East Section

Upon entering the museum you find yourself in the main hall with its display of late Minoan III caskets from the areas around Chania and Rethymnon (Armeni and Apodoulou). To the left are finds from the prefecture's prehistoric caves and from Minoan settlements such as Nerokourou, Vrysses, and Kydonia. Among the noteworthy finds from excavations in Minoan Kydonia, on Kastelli hill inside the old city of Chania, are the tablets with Linear A and B writing and the clay seal, known as

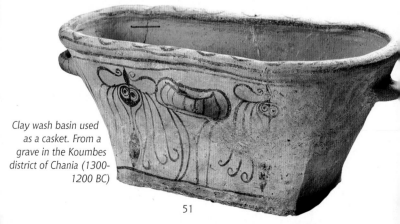

Clay wash basin used as a casket. From a grave in the Koumbes district of Chania (1300-1200 BC)

51

Clay vase (pyxis) depicting a guitar player. From a chamber tomb in the Kiliari Kalyva-Aptera region (1300-1200 BC)

The West Section

Passing through the area with the caskets you arrive at the main area of the west section with its collection of sculpture (statuary, grave stelae, inscriptions), Roman mosaics from the town of Chania, and the numismatic collection. The sculpture collection, dating mostly from the the Master Impression, depicting a regal male figure at the top of a palace-like structure. To the right of the main hall are displays of objects from the late Minoan III cemeteries and graves discovered within the Chania city limits and on its outskirts.

Head of a clay figurine, city of Chania, late 4th c. BC

sites throughout the prefecture (Aptera, Falassarna, Tarra, Lissos), as well as the collections of glass vases and jewelry.

Statue of Artemis from Menies

Hellenistic and Roman times, comes from archeological sites throughout the prefecture.
In the other areas of the west section visitors can admire finds from the Geometric period, groups of finds from major archeological

Bust of the Roman emperor Hadrian, Diktaean sanctuary, 2nd c. AD

The Byzantine and Late Byzantine Collection

The Chania Byzantine and Late Byzantine Collection is housed in the Venetian church of San Salvatore on the northwest tip of the harbor, next to the cavalier of the same name, at 82 Theotokopoulou Street. On display are finds from the 13th Ephorate of Byzantine Antiquities and privately donated objects that shed valuable light on the history and artistic production of the prefecture from Early Christian times through the Turkish occupation.

In this well organized exhibition with its wealth of visual and descriptive

Saint George. Painting by Emmanuel Tzanes (1660-1680)

material, one can admire important icons, frescos, sculpture, architectural fragments, mosaics, ceramics, and coins.

- ■ EARLY CHRISTIAN ARCHITECTURAL SCULPTURE AND GRAVE INSCRIPTIONS
- ■ EARLY CHRISTIAN MOSAIC FLOOR
- ■ MIDDLE AND LATE BYZANTINE FRESCOS
- ■ MIDDLE BYZANTINE ICONS
- ■ VENETIAN PERIOD SCULPTURE
- ■ COINS
- ■ MINIATURES
- ■ CERAMICS

The Historical Archives of Crete

The Historical Archives of Crete, which are part of the National Archives, are housed in a neoclassical building at 20 Ioannis Sfakianaki Street. The purpose of archives is to collect, record and preserve all heirlooms and accounts having to do with Cretan

history. To date, some 700,000 historical documents have been amassed including correspondence from the Cretan Rebellions, archives belonging to important figures, material from the German occupation, all the Cretan press, etc. The museum also has a large library and a collection of folk art.

The Naval Museum

The Naval Museum was founded in 1973 and is housed in a building at the entrance to the Firkas. Its exhibits include models of ships, paintings, archival photographs, naval mementos, finds of underwater archaeology, etc. The institution's basic aim is to disseminate Cretan maritime tradition.

The War Museum

The War Museum is located next to the Chania Municipal Gardens at the junction of Sfakianaki and

Tzanakaki Streets. The collection is made up mostly of photographs and mementos from the major wars of the 20th century.

Hours of Archeological Sites, Museums, and Monuments

1 October to 31 March
Monday: closed
Tuesday-Sunday: 08.30-15.00

29 April to 30 September
Daily: 08.30-17.00

Closed
6th January, Clean Monday, Holy Saturday, Easter Monday, Feast of the Holy Ghost, 28th October, 1st January, 25th March, Good Friday (until 12.00), Easter Sunday, 1st May, 24-25 December:

The Naval Museum

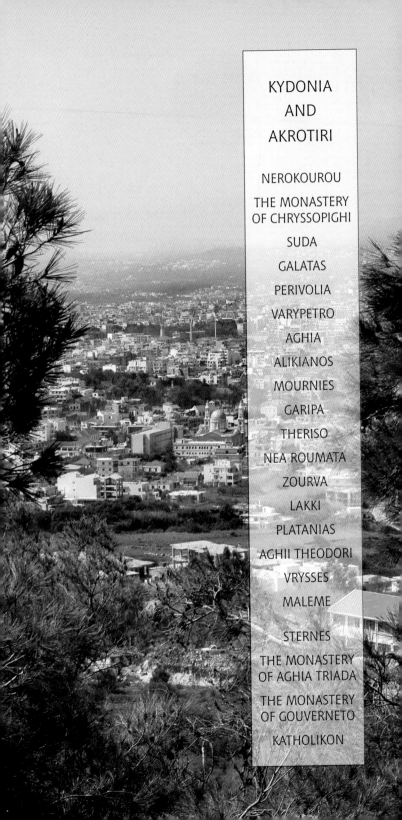

KYDONIA

Nerokourou

The village of Nerokourou is found 5 kilometers outside of Chania at the turn-off for Suda. In addition to the 16th century church of Aghii Saranta, the site of Metohi Aghios Georgios in this area has yielded highly significant archeological finds. This settlement dates from the period of transition from the Neolithic age to Early Minoan. Another settlement discovered here, dating from the end of the Middle Minoan period, was organized into neighborhoods and contained grand two-story homes with paved courtyards. Recent research informs us that the settlement continued to exist into the Late Minoan III period.

The Monastery of Chryssopighi

Three kilometers along the Chania-Suda road lies the Monastery of Zoodochou Pighi or Chryssopighi, which must have been founded sometime between 1550 and 1560. A drawing dated 1745 depicts the monastery and its landholdings. Chryssopighi is a monastery resembling a fort. Its katholikon or main church is situated in the center of an

interior courtyard, while the cells and auxiliary rooms are in structures built around the perimeter of the property. Beyond the building complex are its large fields of olive orchards and vineyards. The monastery's main gate contains the coat of arms of its founder, Ioannis Hartofylakas, a doctor who renovated an earlier monastery that was situated in the same place. The katholikon we see today was built in the 17th century but the porch is a mid-19th century addition. The monastery's museum contains precious

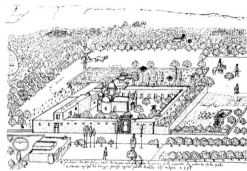

The Monastery of Chryssopighi in a sketch by Plakas in 1745

sacramental vessels, manuscripts, and icons dating from the 15th, 16th, and 17th centuries. The monastery suffered the considerable ravages of time, particularly during the Turkish years, but was renovated in the early 19th century. A century later, however, it found itself on the brink of decline. It was then, around 1970, that a group of nuns took it over and revived it by converting it into a convent.

Suda (settlement, port, island/fort)

The town of Suda, located 6.5 kilometers from Chania eastwards on the road to Rethymnon, runs along the south shore of Suda Bay. Accounts of the Venetian period tell us that this region once contained only salt-beds, which the Turks called tuzla. Thus the entire region was given the name Tuzla. When the salt-beds dried up in 1870 the Turks commenced building a new settlement.
The word suda comes from the Latin and means "entrenchment,"

as mentioned by the English traveler Pashley. The rapid growth of the modern settlement is obviously due to the exploitation of the bay as a port. It is, in fact, one of the largest natural harbors in the Mediterranean. Besides the settlement, the name Suda is also given to the bay and the tiny island inside it. A bit further

Myth has it that the name "Lefkai," or "White," was given to the islands after the contest between the Sirens and the Muses in Aptera. When the Sirens were defeated, they shed their wings from their shoulders, became "lefkai" or "white," and jumped into the sea. The "Lefkai (White) Islands" emerged in the place where they entered the water.

Suda (Basilicata, 1618)

away is another islet. During antiquity the island group was called Lefkai.

The Venetians subsequently named the smaller of the two Isle of Rabbits (Scoglio de Conigli) and the larger one Suda. A fort was built on Suda to prevent entry into the bay, which proved to be one of the most important Venetian fortifications. It remained in Venetian

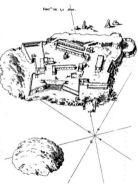

control until 1715, a number of years after the Turks had taken over the rest of Crete. By Basilicata's accounts, construction began on the fort, which was built on the foundations of an earlier one, in 1570. It took only three years to complete. It was equipped with 44 canons and its ramparts had bastions on all sides except on the east, which was naturally fortified by its craggy rocks. Basilicata

Galatas in the early 20th century

himself informs us that the fort contained munitions depots, cisterns, soldiers' quarters, the residences of the proveditore or Lookout and the Military Commander, a cathedral or duomo, and two other churches.

Galatas

One of Chania's most beautiful western suburbs, Galatas is located 8 kilometers from the city. Ruins of Early/Middle Minoan settlements have been discovered on a coastal hillock at Psathi and in the neighboring village of Stalos. Accounts tell us that, under Venetian rule, Galatas was a settlement with 215 registered inhabitants. It was from this location that the Turks began their siege of Chania in 1645. During the years of Turkish occupation Galatas was a strategic

oint from which the rebels organized their campaigns. Galatas also played an important role in World War II. One of the most heroic conflicts, not only in the Battle of Crete but in the entire war, was played out here, as witnessed by the famous monument to the fallen erected on this spot.

Perivolia

Four kilometers south of the city of Chania is the suburb Perivolia (gardens). As its name declares, it was once filled with gardens and still is to a large extent today. This area also contains the cave of **Mamelukos**, where archeological excavators have unearthed middle-Minoan period pottery. The cave is especially interesting for its stalactites.

Varypetro

The village of Varypetro is approximately 8 kilometers south of the city of Chania, just off the main road to Alikianos and Omalos. The lush green landscape is the product of the area's

Kastellos

abundant natural springs, which also provide Chania with its water supply.
What may be the earliest Minoan settlement in the Chania prefecture has been discovered on the hill of **Dembla**. The site contains rudimentary single-room houses with roofs made of clay and branches.
The 250-meter high hill of **Kastellos** in the same region offers a view of the entire Chania plain and the north coast

as far as the Spatha promontory. This explains why the site contains the remains of a fortified citadel. The wall is Byzantine, except for the lower sections, which belong to more ancient times. Hellenistic and Roman period buildings have been discovered inside the citadel itself, which, combined with the wall, has led certain scholars to identify this site as ancient Kydonia. However, archeological evidence of the existence of ancient Kydonia underneath the modern city of Chania allows room for the identification of this particular site as one of cities – Polihna, Pergamos or Keraia - testified as being adjacent to Chania.

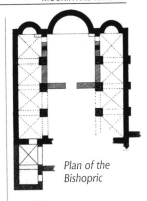

Plan of the Bishopric

Aghia

Aghia is located 10 kilometers outside Chania on the road to Omalos. The name most likely comes from the Arabic word aia, meaning water. Indeed, there are many natural springs throughout the entire region that also supply the city of Chania with its water. During the Middle Byzantine period the bishopric of Kydonia moved to Aghia. Gerola informs us that the **episcopal church** of Our Lady (the Panaghia) was constructed on

The Bishopric of Aghia in a photograph by Gerola

Alkyon

top of the ruins of an earlier church. This is evident if one examines the north wall and the architectural fragments built into it. The new cathedral was designed as a three-aisle basilica. Each of the side aisles was divided into four chapels, topped with pointed vaults. A two-room narthex was added later on. Again by Gerola's account,

the church was rebuilt many times and thus the chapels were roofed in the simplest fashion. One very good reason to go to Aghia is to visit the rich wildlife habitat at the **lake**/dam of the same name. In fact, the Aghia wetlands are considered the most important in Crete. The lake's dense vegetation is home to moorhens, ducks, geese, and swans, which multiply considerably over the winter. When the weather is especially cold many varieties of geese, such as greylag geese and bean geese, land and take refuge on Lake Aghia. As for swans, you could say that Aghia is a swan's paradise with its lush vegetation and abundant food supply. Concerning the lake's flora, there are three basic categories of plants: those that grow on the banks, those that float in the water with deep roots in the lake bottom, and those that float with very shallow roots. The lake is also heaven for birds. If you have

both patience and desire, you can observe hundreds of species depending on the season.

Crag Martins in the winter, herons in the spring, herring gulls in the summer, and white wagtails in the fall are only a few of the surprises that the lake holds in store.

The water, too, is home to hundreds of frogs, turtles, and eels.

Alikianos

Twelve kilometers south of Chania on the road to Omalos is the large village of Alikianos, situated in a huge basin dense with orange groves. The **Keritis River**, called Iardanos in antiquity, flows through the region. Besides the breathtaking sight of the orange groves, it is worth visiting the village that was the

Aghios Georgios

Ruins of the Da Molin castle

fife of the famous **Da Molin** family during Venetian rule. The Da Molins built their castle here in 1229, when the first member of the family landed in Crete. Today, the ruins of this majestic complex survive among the orange groves, close to the rural road that runs through the village. In addition to the Villa Da Molin in Alikianos, one should also visit the Byzantine church of **Aghios Georgios** (St. George) in the village, quite near the villa. Reconstructed and restored, this cruciform church dates from 1243 and contains frescos from 1440 by the well-known icon painter Pavlos

Provatas.
Also, one should not miss the church of **Ai Kyr Yannis** on the outskirts of the village, along the road to the village of Koufos. This recently reconstructed church is cruciform with a dome, and is covered with frescos from various periods. It dates from the 14th century and is believed to have been built on top of an earlier church dedicated to the Zoodohou Pighi (Source of Life), built by Saint John the Foreigner in 1004. The new church was named Ai Kyr Yannis in his honor.

*An interesting tradition associated with Alikianos and the **Da Molin** family is preserved by the author Zambelios in his novel "Cretan Weddings", based on Trivan's chronicle. The story has it that the Cretan rebel George Kantanoleos visited the nobleman Francesco Da Molin as soon as he arrived in the village of Alikianos. The reason for the visit was to ask for the hand of Da Molin's daughter as his son's bride. Da Molin accepted and decided that the wedding should take place in Alikianos, at the church of Aghios Georgios. Da Molin, however, notified the central Venetian administration in Chania and on the wedding day 200 men gathered in the village. At the party, Kantanoleos' guests got so drunk that the Venetians easily rounded them up and brought them before the Venetian authorities. Kantanoleos himself, his sons, and all their henchmen were strung up on the spot. The rest of the guests followed; some were hanged, and others were imprisoned.*

Ai Kyr Yannis

Mournies

The suburb of Mournies is 4 kilometers south of the city of Chania. It is famous as the birthplace of **Eleftherios Venizelos**, whose house is now a museum. The name of this lush green region evidently comes from the profusion of mulberry (*mouria*) trees growing here. Besides its greenery and luxurious estates, the area also contains a number of churches and monasteries.

The birthplace of Eleftherios Venizelos

Just outside the village is the **Monastery of Aghia Kyriaki**, which was a metochi or dependency of the Chryssopighi Monastery in the 17th century, and the **Monastery of Aghios Eleftherios**, where Eleftherios Venizelos is said to have been baptized. It is worth making a stop at the **Sinaitic Monastery of Aghia Triada** (Holy Trinity), located on the road to Perivolia. The monastery contains an olive press, convincing proof that it supplied the Sinai Monastery with olive oil.

Monastery of Aghia Triada

Garipa

Slightly the south of Peribolia and Mournies is the settlement of Garipa, which achieved fame during the Venetian occupation. It is near the historical village of **Boutsounaria,**

famous as the meeting place of Cretan rebels in the 19th century,

and certain scholars believe it to be one and the same place. The general environs of the village hold a plethora of Byzantine churches.

Just outside the village, on the carriage road, is the church of **Aghios Georgios**. Despite its ruined state, its fine architecture and

frescos still provoke admiration.

Theriso

Theriso is located 15 kilometers south of Chania on the northern slopes of the Lefka (White) Mountains. In addition to its natural beauty and delicious dairy products, Theriso is historically significant for the major role it played in the Cretan rebellions of the 19th century.

The most important event associated with Theriso is the **revolt of** **Venizelos**, whose mother came from this very village. It was here that the March 1905 revolt against Prince George began,

*The road to the village passes through the famous **Therisan Gorge**. The gorge is 6 kilometers long and its bed densely wooded with plane, olive, and locust trees.*

an event eventually leading to George's resignation and paving the way for the union of Crete with the rest of Greece. Theriso was also the birthplace of the **Halides** brothers, 19th century rebels.

*About 2.5 kilometers north of Theriso is the **Elliniko cave** or Kato Sarakina, where seashells from the Neolithic, Minoan, and Geometric periods have been found. To visit the cave all you have to do is park your car on the main road and follow the well designed wooden stairs up the mountain slope.*

The statue of Eleftherios Venizelos in Theriso

ΕΛΕΥΘΕΡΙΟΣ ΒΕΝΙΖΕΛΟΣ
ΘΕΡΙΣΟ 1905

Nea Roumata

Nea Roumata is located 26 kilometers south of Chania.
In addition to the beautiful verdant

landscape extending as far as the neighboring villages of Prasses and Hosti, the Nea Roumata valley is also the site of an important archeological discovery. In 1980 a small Early-Minoan period **tholos tomb** was unearthed. The tomb, which is built of stone, contained a skeleton in a crouched position and two pots.

Meskla

The village of Meskla is 20 kilometers south of Chania. It can be reached by taking the Chania – Omalos road and turning left at the crossroads to Fournes. It is located on the northern slopes of the Lefka Mountains in a verdant landscape. Meskla is worth visiting not only for its natural beauty but also for its archeological interest. According to the

historian Polybius, Meskla was the site of the ancient city **Keraia**, which most likely gave its name to the River Keritis that originates in the mountains nearby. Remains of the ancient

settlement, mostly its walls, which are Cyclopean in some spots, as well as some portable objects have been discovered in the village.
In the lower part of the village is the church of **Sotiras Christos** (Christ the Savior), a single-aisle church with a narthex and frescos

According to the foundation inscription, the frescos in the central nave date from 1303 and the narthex from 1471.

painted by Theodoros Daniil and his nephew Mikhail Veneris. Near the south exit out of town is the large church of the Panaghia (Our Lady). This church

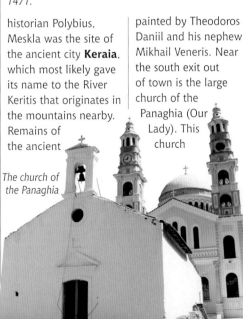

The church of the Panaghia

was built on top of an early Christian basilica, and one can see remnants of a mosaic floor with geometric designs, dating from the 5th or 6th century AD. Small column capitals have been incorporated into the south wall of the new church.

Meskla

Zourva

One can reach the village of Zourva, 27 kilometers from Chania, from either Theriso or Meskla. Perched on the sheer north slopes of the Lefka Mountains, this village will certainly impress the viewer with its breathtaking landscape.

Lakki

The village of Lakki is located 24 kilometers south of Chania on the rural road to Omalos. It is worth the trip for the wonderful view of the Lefka Mountains. By Pashley's accounts, the mountainous character of Lakki was responsible for its inhabitants distinguishing themselves in the war. But despite their so-called "robust appearance," he claims that the natives of Lakki do not resemble those of Sfakia, who are tall and regal. Pashley notes that Lakki and Theriso, a village just to the east, are the main villages in the region known as Riza that includes the north slopes of the Lefka Mountains and southern Apokoronas. As the name implies, this region was most likely the site of the ancient city of **Rizinia**.

War Memorial in Lakkos

Lakki

Platanias

Ten kilometers outside Chania along the road to Kastelli is the seaside settlement of Platanias. Developed for tourism, its extensive facilities and sandy beach offer visitors an opportunity to swim and relax. The name comes from the **River Platanias** or **Iardanos** at whose mouth it is built. Although the settlement is on the sea, it is built on a rocky cliff that ensures a wonderful view of the sea and the little islet of Aghii Theodori or Thodorou. According to Pashley, this was very likely the site of the ancient city of Pergamos, which Pliny situates between Kydonia and Kissamos. On the other hand, other scholars situate Pergamos in either Vrysses or Grimbiliana.

Aghii Theodori

This is the rocky islet in the Gulf of Chania, just opposite Platanias. As in antiquity, when it was known as **Akition** (= place unsuited to habitation), it is uninhabited today as well.

> The Venetians called the island San Theodoro and built two forts on it to protect the shore of Platanias across the way. The lower of the two structures was the fort of Aghios Frangiskos; the higher one was Aghios Theodoros, also called Turluru. The forts were completed in 1585, but were unable to withstand the first attack of the Turks in 1645. To avoid surrendering to the Turks, Giuliani, the heroic commander, set fire to the fort, blowing it up along with all its soldiers and any Turks who had landed there.

Thodorou, 17th century

was built on top of an early Christian basilica, and one can see remnants of a mosaic floor with geometric designs, dating from the 5th or 6th century AD. Small column capitals have been incorporated into the south wall of the new church.

Meskla

Zourva

One can reach the village of Zourva, 27 kilometers from Chania, from either Theriso or Meskla. Perched on the sheer north slopes of the Lefka Mountains, this village will certainly impress the viewer with its breathtaking landscape.

Lakki

The village of Lakki is located 24 kilometers south of Chania on the rural road to Omalos. It is worth the trip for the wonderful view of the Lefka Mountains. By Pashley's accounts, the mountainous character of Lakki was responsible for its inhabitants distinguishing themselves in the war. But despite their so-called "robust appearance," he claims that the natives of Lakki do not resemble those of Sfakia, who are tall and regal. Pashley

notes that Lakki and Theriso, a village just to the east, are the main villages in the region known as Riza that includes the north slopes of the Lefka Mountains and southern Apokoronas. As the name implies, this region was most likely the site of the ancient city of **Rizinia**.

War Memorial in Lakkos

Lakki

Platanias

Ten kilometers outside Chania along the road to Kastelli is the seaside settlement of Platanias. Developed for tourism, its extensive facilities and sandy beach offer visitors an opportunity to swim and relax. The name comes from the **River Platanias** or **Iardanos** at whose mouth it is built. Although the settlement is on the sea, it is built on a rocky cliff that ensures a wonderful view of the sea and the little islet of Aghii Theodori or Thodorou. According to Pashley, this was very likely the site of the ancient city of Pergamos, which Pliny situates between Kydonia and Kissamos. On the other hand, other scholars situate Pergamos

Aghii Theodori

This is the rocky islet in the Gulf of Chania, just opposite Platanias. As in antiquity, when it was known as **Akition** (= place unsuited to habitation), it is uninhabited today as well.

in either Vrysses or Grimbiliana.

The Venetians called the island San Theodoro and built two forts on it to protect the shore of Platanias across the way. The lower of the two structures was the fort of Aghios Frangiskos; the higher one was Aghios Theodoros, also called Turluru. The forts were completed in 1585, but were unable to withstand the first attack of the Turks in 1645. To avoid surrendering to the Turks, Giuliani, the heroic commander, set fire to the fort, blowing it up along with all its soldiers and any Turks who had landed there.

Thodorou, 17th century

Vrysses

You will find the route to the village of Vrysses (16 kilometers from Chania) inside the village of Platanias. An ancient settlement on a citadel has been found there with a marvelous view of Platanias and the valley of Alikianos. This walled settlement shows traces of habitation from as early as Neolithic and Minoan times. Certain scholars claim that this was the site of the ancient city of Pergamos. Pergamos, which according to tradition was founded by either Agamemnon or Aeneas, was built on a hilltop that some, like Pashley, identify as the rocky hill of Platanias and others as Grimbiliana

or Vrysses.

Maleme

Maleme, located 16 kilometers outside Chania along the national road to Kastelli, is famous mostly because of the Battle of Crete. Maleme had an airstrip, built prior to World War II, which was taken over by German paratroopers.

Although it has been developed as a resort, Maleme is also of archeological interest. A 1966 excavation in the northern section

The tholos tomb

revealed a Late Minoan III **tholos tomb**. The tomb has a corridor with constructed walls and is 13.80 meters

The German Cemetery

The graves of Eleftherios and Sophocles Venizelos on Akrotiri

AKROTIRI

The peninsula of Akrotiri (= promontory), east of the city of Chania, now called **Melehas**, was known as **Kyamon** in antiquity. The region must have been inhabited from Neolithic times since evidence from that period has been found on its northwest side. The Chania airport is built on the promontory's central plateau. Akrotiri contains numerous villages, historic monasteries and exceptional caves.

Sternes

Sternes is on the southeast part of Akrotiri, 14 kilometers from the city of Chania, and has a wonderful view of Suda Bay. A farmstead from the Late Minoan IIIC period was discovered near the village. On the inlet just below the village is the ancient seaside town of **Minoa**, which was one of the two ports of Aptera (the other was in Kissamos in the Kalami-Kalyves region). Its position corresponds to the point just across from **Marathi**. Docks, cisterns, and Roman-era structures have been discovered in the area around Minoa.

Marathi

The Monastery of Aghia Triada Mourtari or Giancarolo

Located 16 kilometers from Chania in the northwest part of Akrotiri, this monastery dates from the 17th century. It was built by Jeremiah and Laurentio Giancarolo, two Venetian monks who had embraced Orthodoxy. In essence, the Giancarolo brothers

renovated an older monastery that belonged to the equally wealthy Mourtari family. It is said, in fact, that since they were the offspring of a noble family they got their plans for the

monastery from Mount Athos. Work began in 1612 and the major portion of the monastery was completed then, except for the church dome, which was added much later in 1843. You approach the monastery through an amazing landscape of olive

As Pashley informs us, there is a chapel on the east corner, and a cemetery in front of it.

trees and grapevines. After passing through a majestic stand of cypress trees you reach the square in front of the well-preserved monastery. The size of complex is extremely impressive, particularly its grand entryway. The building façade has three stories, two of which are complete,

and a mezzanine. The entrance gate topped with a tall bell tower is a direct reference to European architectural prototypes of the 17th century. In the center of the courtyard is the church with its two chapels, one dedicated to the Zoodocho Pighi (Source of Life) and the other to Saint John the

and the auxiliary rooms are housed around the perimeter of the flagstone courtyard, underneath which are cisterns to collect rainwater. The monastery's museum contains manuscripts and important portable icons from the 15th, 16th, 17th, and subsequent centuries.

Theologian. Its façade is decorated with Doric columns. Its lintel contains an inscription and the entablature the letters ΒΓVΘΤΠ. To the left and right of the entrance to the porch are Greek and Latin inscriptions, respectively, and the date 1634. The cells, the refectory

The Monastery of Gouvernetos or Gdernetos

This monastery is located 5 kilometers north of Aghia Triada Monastery. The road there goes through a small gorge, but the landscape is relatively barren and has mostly shrubbery. In front of the monastery is

a large square. The visitor is immediately aware that this is a fortress-type complex with a square tower on each of its four corners. It has a rectangular plan with an inner courtyard dominated by a domed, cruciform church dedicated to the Virgin. The façade of the church and its bell tower are richly ornamented, particularly the lowest zone with its projecting column bases. The zone directly above this is especially noteworthy for both the masks/figures at the base of each column as well as the carved decoration in the interstices.

Our Lady (Panaghia) the Arkoudiotissa & Katholikon

The katholikon of this monastery is located to the north of the Gouvernetos Monastery and can be reached only by foot, following the path from the monastery's garden. Along the path one can see the caves where ascetics lived during Byzantine times. Midway along the path you will arrive at the cave of the **"Arkoudiotissa"** (= Lady Bear), so-named because inside the cave is a stalagmite that looks just like a bear bending over to drink. This cave, which appears to have been used for worship since antiquity, continued to be so in Christian times and was dedicated to the Arkoudiotissa Panaghia.

After a half-hour hike and a descent of some 140 steps at the end of the route, you arrive at the katholikon of the abandoned monastery, which is believed to have been founded in the 5th or 6th century by Saint John the Hermit. It is built into the vertical walls of the cliff and faces north. A little stone bridge acts as the front yard of what in essence is a church carved into the rock face with a uniquely designed entrance that has a pedimental top and a rose window. Equally interesting is the gate leading to the monastery's courtyard, which also has Renaissance features based

on designs by the Renaissance architect Sebastiano Serlio. The view and landscape is so striking that Pashley himself writes characteristically, "I cannot contemplate any other landscape more suited to those desiring to live far from mankind and close to God."

The Katholikon by Pashley

APOKORONAS

VAMOS

GEORGIOUPOLI

LAKE KOURNAS

DRAMIA

VRYSSES

STYLOS

KYRIAKOSELIA

KALYVES

ALMYRIDA

KALAMI

APTERA

APOKORONAS

Most of Apokoronas comprises a plain southeast of the massif of the Lefka Mountains. It extends on its northeast side to form the Drapanos promontory. Basilicata described Apokoronas as a mountainous yet very fertile region. The **Kiliaris River** runs through it from its source in the Lefka Mountains to its outlet in Suda Bay. In antiquity this river was called **Pyknos** (=dense) because of the dense vegetation along its banks. According to Pashley, the name Apokoronas comes from that of the ancient city of **Ippokoronas or Ippokoronion**, which is also cited by Strabo.

One opinion has it that this city was located in the modern village of **Nippos**, where a settlement has been discovered in Kavousia. Another opinion, however,

CASTEL APICORONO

places it on the coast around Castel Apicorono. A fortress during Venetian times, the **Castel Apicorono** was also the seat of the castellania. The castle is located on a rocky elevation to the east of the modern village of Kalyves, near Almyrida (Kastelli). It is not clear whether it was built by Pescatore or by the Venetians at a later date. It fell to the Turks in 1646.

Vamos

Vamos, a chief village in the interior of Apokoronas, is 26 kilometers from Chania and the capital of the district. In reality it is a town with many public services and infrastructure. Located

north of the national road, it demarcates a region of remarkably picturesque villages largely untouched by tourism that extend the length of the Drapanos promontory. In addition to the lush green landscape and stone houses, this is the place where the visitor encounters Cretan tradition in all its glory.

Georgioupoli

The coastal settlement of Georgioupoli is located 43 kilometers east of Chania on the national road to Rethimnon. It lies on the inlet of Almyros bay, and archeological evidence identifies

it as the ancient city of **Amfimala or Amfimalion**, the ancient port of Lappa, which is today's Argyroupoli. Nowadays, Georgioupoli is a tourist resort with many hotels, taverns and exciting nightlife.

Lake Kournas

Inland and south of Georgioupoli, about 47 kilometers from Chania, is Lake Kournas, near the village of the same name. Crete's only lake, Kournas is quite large, with a perimeter of 3.5 kilometers. By Pashley's account, this area held **Korion** and a temple of Athena.

Today Korion is located in the general area of Metohi and Kavalos settlements. The lake used to be called **Korisia** after Korion, and reportedly was filled with eels. Nowadays it is considered one of the major tourist attractions in all of Crete and it teems with life in the summertime. The most beautiful time to visit the lake, however, is in the winter. Then you can enjoy the enchanting landscape with its snowcapped mountains mirrored in its crystalline waters in

total peace and quiet.

Dramia

This village, built along the Mouselas River, is located 45 kilometers east of Chania on the border with Rethymnon prefecture. Given its name, it must have been the site of the ancient city of **Hydramia**, described by the scholar Stefanos Vyzantios. Hydramia was the port of Lappa. Its enormous sandy beach has made it a popular holiday resort today.

Vrysses

On the right hand side, 33 kilometers along the Chania-Rethymnon road, is the chief village of Vrysses. As its name (= springs) denotes, the village has abundant natural springs due to the Vryssanos River, which runs through it. The village is in two sections, built on either

side of the river and connected by a bridge that forms the locus of the village's main square. The lush green landscape with its tall plane trees entices the visitor to stop and admire the view. You can then have a cool drink of water and try some of the traditional yogurt and hand-kneaded bread in one of the local cafes. The rural road to Sfakia begins at Vrysses.

Yogurt and honey. Don't leave Vrysses without trying it.

Pangratium maritimum. Often seen on the beach in Dramia

Stylos

Located near the village of Samonas, Stylos has remarkable natural beauty and abundant water from the Kiliaris River. It is the site of an important early Minoan settlement that, according to archeological evidence, was abandoned during the late Minoan IIIC

Minoan structures in Stylos

period.
At the northern end of the village is the church of Our Lady, the **Panaghia Zerviotissa or Monastira**, which dates from the 11th/ 12th century and has a four-column domed cruciform plan. Nearby is the church of **Aghios Ioannis** (St. John), which was the metochi or dependency of the monastery of Saint John the Theologian of Patmos. Its frescos date it between 1271-1280. It has two aisles and a narthex on its west side.

as medieval, survive on **Kastelli Hill**. The fortress is named Aghios Nikolaos after the Byzantine church inside it. This fortress played a significant role when the Venetians arrived on the island. For six long years it was headquarters for the Byzantine militia, surrendering to the Venetians only in 1236. Although it is located in an isolated place, the fort had strategic importance because it could monitor all of Suda Bay.
The church of **Aghios Nikolaos** is a single-aisle basilica with an impressive dome. Its frescos, dating from c. 1230, are of exceptional significance because they are connected to the artistic tradition of Nicaea.

Kyriakoselia

Kyriakoselia is 31 kilometers from

Chania and very close to Stylos. The ruins of a wall, which Pashley characterizes

The Byzantine church of Aghios Nikolaos

Kalyves

17 kilometers east of Chania is the coastal settlement of Kalyves. Its long stretch of sandy beach has made this a popular tourist destination. Today it is a beautiful, modern resort offering every comfort and convenience.

On a hill just to the east are the ruins of **Castel Apicorono**, identified by some scholars as the location of the ancient city of **Ippokoronion**. According to ancient Greek historian and geographer Strabo, Kissamos was located in the area between Kalyves and Kalami. **Kissamos** and Minoa were the two ports of ancient Aptera.

Almyrida

At Almyrida, just east of Kalyves, visitors can enjoy a beautiful beach and also admire the ruins of one of Crete's major early Christian basilicas, found at the entrance to the village.

The **basilica**, whose exceptional mosaic from its central nave still survives, had three aisles, a transept, and a narthex. It dates from the 6th century AD.

Kalami
Itzedin Fortress

The coastal settlement of Kalami is 18 kilometers east of Chania. On his map of Spiaggia del Apicorno (Beach of Apokoronas), Basilicata depicted and named the position of a spring in Kalami (**Calami Fontana**) along this coast, the remains of which are still visible. Although Basilicata cited the need for a fortress in this area to better protect the port of Suda, only the Turks built a castle, which was completed in 1872. Called **Itzedin** after the son

Itzedin Fortress (Ilustrated Lomndon News)

of Abdul Aziz, the fortress was built on the hill on a spot called Podomouri, noted by Basilicata as Podomuria on his map. After the Turks left the island, the fortress was used as a prison and is still in excellent condition to this day.

Hellenistic period sanctuary

Aptera

The ancient city of Aptera is located just south of Kalami and 15 kilometers east of Chania, on an elevation with a spectacular view of Suda Bay. Pashley, in 1834, was the first to identify the ruins on the hill of Paliokastro as Aptera, substantiating his claims with coins discovered in the ancient city. The city's ports were Minoa, near today's

Marathi, and Kissamos, which is situated between Kalyves and Almyrida. Aptera was in existence by the Minoan era, but finds discovered in the main part of the city date from the Geometric period and after. According to the scholar Stefanos Vyzantios, the city got its name from the Sirens, who when defeated by the Muses in a musical competition, wrenched their wings (= ptera in Greek) from their shoulders and threw them into the sea. **Walls** totaling 4 kilometers in length mark the city's boundaries. The most important monuments of ancient Aptera are contained within these walls and date from various periods. Just to the right when you enter the site, you will see a Hellenistic-period **two-part sanctuary**. Northeast of the sanctuary is the first **theater** belonging to the same era and located beneath the ruins

The Turkish fortress

The cisterns in Aptera by Pashley

of a Roman theater. Also near the theater is a **Doric temple**. The large three-aisle, vaulted **cistern** is also from Roman times. It has been alternately interpreted as a public bathhouse or a wheat granary. A large number of **graves** have been discovered to the west of the city. They date from the Geometric period through Roman times. The site also contains the **Monastery of Aghios Ioannis** (Saint John) the Theologian, south of which archeologists have discovered an **early Christian basilica** containing Christian graves under its floor. A plethora of important portable objects have

been unearthed as well – including inscriptions, statues, and pottery – and may be seen in the Chania archaeological museum. But the most important finds of all are the **coins**, since they are what

confirm that Aptera was a great commercial and maritime power. Seventy-six types of coins have been recorded, most of which have a woman's head (perhaps Hera's) and the inscription

ΑΠΤΑΡΑΙΩΝ or ΑΠΤΕΡΑΙΩΝ on the face, and a bearded warrior on the reverse. Aptera appears to have been destroyed by an earthquake in the 7th century AD and it was perhaps then that its inhabitants moved to the area that is now the village of Rakhes. Nevertheless, Aptera received the decisive blow from the Arabs who leveled the city entirely in 823 AD. When the Venetians found the ruins of the ancient city they called it Paliokastro (Old Castle) and built a wall to protect the port of Suda.

Statue found at Aptera

SFAKIA

Stretching across the Lefka Mountains, this region is one of Crete's most mountainous. Samaria also belongs to this geographical department. Surface excavations conducted throughout the entire region in recent years have revealed traces of habitation going back to the Early Minoan period in the mountains. But most the coastal areas such as Frangokastello, Loutro, and Aghia Roumeli appear to have been even more populated.

Apart from the breathtaking Samarian Gorge, celebrated for its unrivaled natural beauty, Sfakia contains a number of smaller but equally beautiful ravines such as those of Imbros and Aradena, and impressive caves. There are also marvelous, picturesque mountain villages that must be visited for a true taste of authentic Cretan tradition.

Traditional woman's dress from Sfakia

In addition to their character, the Sfakians are distinguished for their physical traits, remarked on by all those who pass through these parts. They are said to be tall, slender, blond, with Grecian noses and high foreheads, the true descendents of the original Cretans, the handsomest, most impressive warriors, as well as the best, most dashing dancers in Crete.

The rugged landscape with its sheer, often barren, cliffs was not always that way. The Sfakia mountains were once covered with cypress trees and dense forests. These were gradually stripped away, leaving in their place a harsh yet unique landscape. This landscape is clearly reflected in the nature of the Sfakians themselves, a tough, intractable, and austere people who hold fast to the values and customs of their ancestors. Their most famous trait, however, is their defiance, which explains why the villages of Sfakia did not become castellania during Venetian times, but instead were governed by a *proveditore* or Lookout as a semi-autonomous regime. Nor did the Turks manage to subjugate Sfakia, and the region became the locus of Cretan revolutionary activity.

Askyfou

The best way to reach
Sfakia is to take the
road from Vrysses in the
plains of Apokoronas,
and drive through the
southern part of the
Chania prefecture to
the Libyan Sea. This
route through the
Lefka Mountains offers
travelers many unique
vistas and experiences.
Perhaps the first surprise
is the one awaiting
you when you arrive
in the Askyfou basin,
a vast expanse that
often becomes a lake
in wintertime. This
area contains the
neighborhoods and
small settlements of
Askyfou. At one time,
this narrow pass,
which is the highest
point along the route,
provided the only access
to Sfakia from the
north. For this reason,
this and other places

ruins of a **fortress** on
the top of one of the
surrounding hills. The
Turks built this structure
as part of their defense
plan for dealing with
the Cretan rebellion.
Pashley describes the
natives of Askyfou as
tall and rugged and
most generous with
treating guests to their
roast lamb, wine (which
is exceptional because
the grapes are grown
at a high altitude), and
delicious cheese pie
(tyropita). Writing of
the Sfakian cheese pie,

Sfakian tyropita or cheese pie

which is to this day
unique in Crete, Pashley
says that it was fried
and bursting with a soft
cheese that he equates
with the fine cheese
offered at ancient
sacrifices.

The Turkish fortress

in the area, such as the
plateau of Krapi and
the "Gorge of Katre",
were the sites of major
battles during the
Turkish occupation.
Upon entering the
plateau you will see the

In August of 1821 the inhabitants of Askyfou and
Sfakia chased the Turks off and surrounded them in
the **Gorge of Katre,** where they decimated them,
filling the ravine with Turkish bodies. Pashley passed
through the village 13 years later. Not only did he hear
eyewitness accounts of the incident, but he also saw
with his own eyes the scattered bones along the side
of the road.

Imbros

The village of Imbros, or Nimbros as it is also called, is 4 kilometers south of Askyfou and 56 kilometers from Chania. This is the starting point of the 7-kilometer-long **Imbros Gorge**. One of the most impressive gorges in

Crete, the Imbros flows directly east of Hora Sfakion near the village of Komitades. Its sheer walls reach 300 meters in height, and in some spots the passage is barely 2 meters wide. In addition to its geological interest and unique rock formations, the gorge is dense

Ebenus cretica and on the left bluebells

A quick soft drink in the gorge

with conifers, shrubs, and wildflowers. It takes at least 3 - 3.5 hours to walk the gorge, but the trip is an easy one. Approximately midway through you come upon some Venetian ruins. After that the walls rise up and begin to converge, becoming almost perpendicular. At this point the passage narrows considerably. But even if you don't walk the gorge on foot you can still experience much of its beauty from the carriage road that runs along its western side.

Asfentou Kallikratis Asi Gonia

Just before Imbros is the junction for the easternmost villages of the Sfakia region. Built in the foot of the Lefka Mountains, these villages are rather isolated but very picturesque. Most are abandoned during the winter because of the harsh weather. If you take this route, the first village you come to is Asfentou, 61 kilometers from Chania. Neolithic graffiti attributed to hunters have been discovered in a rocky niche at **Skordilakia** at the entrance to the Asfentian Gorge. The **Asfentian Gorge** is 2.5 kilometers long and terminates in the village of Aghios Nektarios. It is quite difficult to go

The Gorge of Gyparis

through on foot. The village of **Kallikratis**, 4.5 kilometers to the east, is composed of small settlements of stone houses. Turks never inhabited this village, only

Sundial in Kallikratis

managing to occupy it after a fierce struggle in 1770. In 1943 Kallikratis was burned to the ground during World War II. And lastly, this is the starting point of

a **gorge** that is part of the E4 European Trail network. The 4-kilometer gorge, which ends at the village of Patsianos, is very easy to walk and takes about 2 – 2.5 hours. Also northeast of Kallikratis is the mountain village of **Asi Gonia**, 61.5 kilometers from Chania and 35 kilometers from Rethymnon. "Asi" in Arabic means gallantry, and the village obviously got this name because of its defiant inhabitants who wreaked terror among their conquerors. The area is densely vegetated especially in the eastern part near the

village of Argyroupoli, with its breathtaking gorge filled with plane trees and the **Gyparis Bridge**.

On April 23rd, Saint George's Day, it is customary in this region for the

Bell Tower in Asi Gonia

shepherds to bring their herds to church to be blessed by the priest. After the Liturgy, milk is boiled in large pots and distributed among the congregation.

Frangokastello

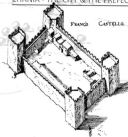

FRANCO CASTELLO

Frangokastello

Shortly before the end of the Chania – Vrysses - Hora Sfakion road, the road branches left towards Komitades. It continues eastward and arrives at Frangokastello, approximately 85 kilometers from Chania. This breathtaking seaside spot was named after the castle that is built practically right on top of the sea. The fortress was originally named Aghios Nikitas because of the church nearby, but the locals called it Frangokastello, meaning the castle of the Franks, and that name stuck. With the intention of protecting the area from pirate incursions, construction began on the fortress in 1371. Its completion, however, was much delayed because the Sfakians would not tolerate the existence of any fortification that would monitor them and check their insurgencies. For the most part, this low-lying fortress with no settlement surrounding it never played any significant part in the defense project, and was all but dismantled. Only during the Turkish occupation was there any fighting in this area, and then mostly by the Cretan rebels. It was here that Daskaloyannis was forced in 1770 to surrender to the Turks. The castle has a square plan with towers on its four corners. Over the main gate is a carving of the lion of Saint Mark and the coat of arms of the **Quirini** and **Dolfin**. The ramparts and anything inside it are the vestiges of Turkish modifications.

In 1828 the rebels Tsouderos, Deliyannis and Hadji Michalis Dalianis had assembled in the Frangokastello. While Mustafa was laying siege on Arkadi, he was informed of the rebel assembly and decided to wipe them out. Hadji Michalis Dalianis insisted that the rebels could withstand Mustafa, so he and 600 fighters locked themselves inside the fort. After a 7-day siege and with Dalianis beheaded, the rebels were in a weakened state. But the same was also true for Mustafa, who had lost 600 men. After strong pressure from Sfakia, the Turks released the rebels, destroyed a large part of the fort, and took to their heels. However, the rebellious Cretans were waiting for them on the road and slaughtered them as they retreated. All these bloody incidents have created a host of legends associated with the area around Frangokastello, the most famous of which is that of the Drossoulites (literally "dew shades"). Supposedly, every year, on the dawn of May 18th, a group of shadowy figures appear, dressed in black with swords and helmets. On foot and on horseback, they move from the ruins of the Church of Aghios Haralambos towards the castle. If anyone approaches them, they disappear into the sea. This apparition is called Drossoulites because it occurs with the early morning dew. People believed these are the ghosts of Hadji Michalis Dalianis and his rebels. There are many explanations for this phenomenon. The prevalent one links it to some sort of light refraction, but does not specify how exactly it occurs.

Ascent towards Imbros

Hora Sfakion

The seaside settlement and harbor of Hora Sfakion is located at the end of the rural road that begins at Vrysses of Apokoronas and cuts horizontally across the Chania prefecture.

The region is 62 kilometers from Chania and as you can see from the descriptions of the villages along this route (Vrysses, Askyfou, and Imbros), the area is extremely rich in history and natural beauty. Hora Sfakion is a popular tourist spot largely because of the boats running from Aghia Roumeli at the exit of the Samarian Gorge. Visitors take boats from Aghia Roumeli to Hora Sfakion and from there continue on to Chania or Rethymnon.

Hora Sfakion was organized into neighborhoods and, as Basilicata informs us, its inhabitants were not only involved in livestock but in shipbuilding as well given that the surrounding mountains provided considerable timber. Basilicata depicts the mountains as densely populated but renders only a few buildings and one church on coast, the location of today's Hora Sfakion. On the rocky outcrop further east he depicts the **Castel Sfachia**, a fortress built by the Venetians in 16th century on top of a much earlier one. They called it Sfachia after the name of the region. This was one of the last fortresses the Venetians built on Crete given that they never entirely managed to bring the Sfakia area under submission. As we've already mentioned, Sfakia had never been castellania, but had a Lookout and a semi-autonomous regime. Virtually nothing survives of this fortress today.

Ilingas

You can see the beach of Ilingas on the left-hand side of the road to Anopoli 1 kilometer west of Hora Sfakion. The trail to the **gorge** that leads to the beach starts to the right of the main road. This beautiful trail follows a riverbank dense with cypress trees and takes about 5 hours.

Anopoli

Anopoli is next to Hora Sfakion and 84 kilometers from Chania. A mountain village on the east side of the Kastro peak, Anopoli is built on a small but fertile plateau 600 meters above sea level. As Pashley notes, its chief crops are

its panorama of the sea southwards. From here you can hike down to Loutro, but it is a difficult trail and takes about a half-hour.

In addition to the walls, Roman-era cist graves have also been discovered here.

The Anopoli plateau deserves a visit both for the beautiful

A carpet of anemones in Anopoli

Ancient **Anopoli**, whose port was Phoenix (today's Loutro), was one of the 31 Cretan cities to sign a peace treaty with Eumenes II, King of Pergamum, in 183 BC. By so doing it gained its independence and was able to mint its own coins. Anopoli was a center of Cretan rebel activity during both the Venetian and the Turkish occupations. It was on this very spot that **Daskaloyannis**, in 1770, together with the Sfakian chieftains raised the flag of the revolution. Unfortunately, the leader was killed in a bitter battle inside the village and Anopoli was completely demolished. In the years that followed it was twice rebuilt and twice burned to the ground.

wine grapes, olives, and barley. Nearby are the ruins of the

ancient city of the same name. At **Aghia Ekaterini**, a 15-minute walk from the village, you can see sections of its large wall that was most likely built around the 3rd century BC. Also in the same spot is the church of Aghia Ekaterini with

trip there and for its wonderful view of the south side of the Lefka Mountains and the southern shores of Crete. The plateau is a paradise of wildflowers in the spring and the point of ascent to the higher peaks of the Lefka Mountains.

Aradena

Next you come to the village of Aradena, 15 kilometers west of Hora Sfakion and built on the west side of the gorge of the same name separating it

from Anopoli. You reach this remote, abandoned village by the impressive metal **Vardinoyannis Bridge** connecting the two sides of the gorge. Aradena is located in same place as the ancient city of **Aradin**, where architectural fragments and graves have been found. Unfortunately, Aradena suffered the same fate as Anopoli. Its inhabitants were successful in shipping and the town prospered during the

*East of the village alongside the ravine is the little Byzantine church of **Mikhail Archangelos**, which has a cruciform plan with a dome and a completely painted interior. Dating from the 14th/15th century, it was built on the foundations of an earlier basilica, as evidenced by a section of wall jutting out at its northeast corner.*

The church of the Archangel Michael of Aradena is one of the few in Crete where herdsmen would gather to take oaths and settle cases of livestock theft.

Venetian and Turkish periods. However, it was totally leveled by the Turks after the heroic battles of 1770 and 1867. Aradena's most notable attraction is its **gorge**, which begins in the Lefka Mountains and ends in the bay of "Marmara." As the name implies, the bay is rocky and even has caves.

Those wanting to hike through the ravine must follow the trail through the village. The 7-kilometer hike takes about 3 hours to complete. The trail is considered quite difficult mainly because of one place where you must descend - or ascend if you've come from the opposite direction - a 10-meter sheer cliff on a double metal ladder that has been placed there by the fire department. You'll need appropriate shoes and equipment, and in no circumstances should you attempt to go through the ravine in the rain. It is subject to rockslides. In general, the best route to take is from the sea towards the village. If you decide to do it in the other direction, from Anopoli to Marmara, you'll have to walk an additional hour along the E4 Trail to Loutro, where you take the boat to Hora Sfakion.

The trail leading down to the ravine

Loutro

Loutro is a small seaside settlement west of Hora Sfakion. There is no road, so visitors must take a boat from Hora Sfakion or Aghia Roumeli. Another way to get there is on foot on the 5-kilometer trail from Anopoli. Loutro is the site of the ancient city of **Phoenix**, the harbor of Aradin (today's Aradena) and Anopoli. Phoenix flourished in Roman times. Buondelmondi describes a plethora of ancient ruins, including statuary, column sections, and building stones, while recent excavations have unearthed finds on the western part of the Mouros promontory. The tiny port of Loutro is considered the most sheltered in southern Crete, which enabled the surrounding towns as far back as ancient times to prosper in naval and commercial activities. It was used in uprisings against the Turks and served as a munitions depot during the 1821 revolution. Basilicata also noted the harbor's potential. His drawings depicting large numbers of

Phoenix

galleons anchored there accentuate the harbor's capacity and safety.

Today Loutro is a tourist destination. There is frequent boat service from Hora Sfakion and it is a stop on the boat route from the exit of the Samarian Gorge. It has many guestrooms and taverns, and is a hangout for pleasure boat owners. Besides swimming and recreation, you can also rent a canoe and explore the nearby beaches. You can visit the **church of Sotiras** (i.e. the Savior) with its 14th century frescos or even try hiking the beautiful 5-hour trail to Aghia Roumeli, which passes through pine forests and the Byzantine church of **Aghios Pavlos**.

SAMARIA

The Lefka (White) Mountains & the Samarian Gorge

The Lefka (White) Mountains dominate the landscape of Chania and all of Crete. The massif contains the second highest mountain (2,452 meters) after the Ida (or Psiloritis)

Mountains, whose highest peak, Timios Stavros, is 2,465 meters. It may derive its name from either the snow that covers the mountain all through the winter and often into the summer, or from their white limestone composition.

The Omalos Plateau and the Lefka Mountains

The Lefka Mountains are also called the **Madares**, meaning bare or without vegetation (from the Greek verb "mado" = to denude or to shed). Pahnes, the highest peak in the Lefka Mountains, is one of 57 others in the same mountain range that exceeds 2000 meters. Extending over 45 kilometers, the area is also known for its plateaus, abundant springs, caves, and of course its gorges and ravines.

A series of geological changes and upheavals 10 million years ago led to the breakup of Aegeis, the landmass that joined Southeastern Europe to Western Asia Minor.

The Samarian Gorge was formed later, during the Pleistocene era, 1-2 million years ago, when the island of Crete took its ultimate shape. This geological event encapsulated and preserved a large portion of the plant life of southern Aegeis. Crete's largest, most breathtaking gorge, the Samarian Gorge is located in the southwest Lefka Mountains. It begins at Xyloskalo on the Omalos plateau and ends at the village of Aghia Roumeli, on the shore of the Libyan Sea. In 1962 its majestic beauty and wealth of flora and fauna won it the title of National Park.

The **Omalos Plateau**,

Xyloskalo

at an altitude of 1080 meters, extends to the provinces of Sfakia, Selino, and Kydonia. It has a nearly circular shape. It has a perimeter of about 25 kilometers, a diameter of approximately 4 kilometers, and three approaches: at Neratzoporo on the northeast, Aghios Theodoros on the west, and Xyloskalo. In addition to the small settlement in the center of the plateau, the home of the leader Hadji Mikhail Yannaris, the leader of the Cretan revolt, stands at the point where the plateau starts. The **Samaria Gorge** is 18 kilometers long. It ranges in width

from 3 to 300 meters and in height from 200 to 1000 meters. Surrounding it is a series of peaks

White peonies, endemic to Samaria

including Gigilos (2,085 meters), Volakias (2,116 meters), Pahnes (2,452), Avlimonakas (1,843), and others. Its narrowest point (just 3 meters wide) is at the place known as Portes or Sideroportes (the "doors" or "iron gates"), near the gorge's exit. The Tarreos River runs the entire length of the gorge and derives

its name from the ancient city of Tarra, near Aghia Roumeli. Eleven smaller ravines feed into the gorge and there are times, especially during the

Ag. Nikolaos

winter, when it is completely impassible. The gorge also contains 20 fresh water springs, the most important of which are in Neroutsiko below Xyloskalo, Riza of Sykia, Linoseli on the road from Xyloskalo to Gigilos, Potistiria,

"Portes"

The ibex

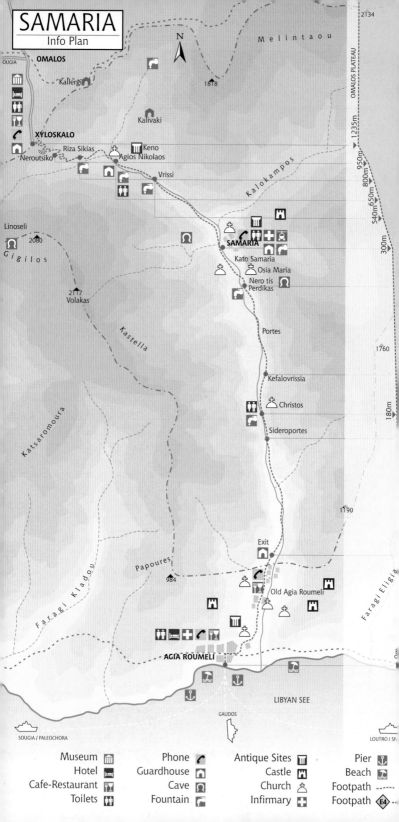

Dracunculus vulgaris

Myrties, Loutsotopos, Vroulia, Kavousi, Vryssi of Perdika, Kefalovryssi, and others.

Before achieving its current fame, the Samarian Gorge was an ecological paradise filled with wild birds, mammals, and abundant plant species, many of which are endemic. Even today you can still find rare plants, like the Cretan maple, dittany, orchids, as well as bearded vultures, booted eagles, and of course the Cretan ibex – known as the kri-kri. Midway along the gorge is the small, now-deserted settlement of Samaria. Originally the home of woodcutters, the region was famous for its cypress trees, which were exported to Egypt and other countries as far back as antiquity. The settlement was abandoned when the gorge became a National Park. There is a Byzantine church, **Osia Maria of Egypt,** and it is quite likely that the name Samaria is a corruption of that name. Nearby is

Donkeys help out when your legs give out

the church of Aghios Nikolaos.

Aghia Roumeli Tarra

At the exit of the Samarian Gorge is the village of Aghia Roumeli, which was abandoned in 1962. It was relocated to its current position on a beautiful white pebble beach where visitors have many choices of rooms and taverns. There is frequent boat service from Aghia Roumeli and the Samarian Gorge to Hora Sfakion. Nature lovers will also enjoy the 5-hour walk

Samaria and archeological remains

Aghia Roumeli

from Aghia Roumeli to Loutro, which takes you through a beautiful pine forest and past the lovely 10th-century church of Aghios Pavlos. This was the site of the ancient city of **Tarra**, where according to mythology the god Apollo and his twin sister Artemis sought refuge after killing the Python at Delphi. According to the Greek chronicler

Pausanias, it was there at the house of the poet Karmanoras that Apollo mated with the nymph Akakkalida. Apollo was worshipped in Tarra and temples were built in his honor there. Buondelmondi saw the ruins of these temples among which were many fragments of female statues, some of which he assumed

The Turkish fortress

to be dedicated to Artemis or to Aphrodite. Tarra was very independent and had its own coins that depicted a wild goat on one side and a honeybee

on the other. Recent excavations have ascertained that the city was continuously inhabited from the Classical period to Roman times, but ceased in the Early Christian period. Cist graves and the remains of glassworks have been found at the site.

The Eligias Gorge

Another, even more impressive but much less known gorge runs through the Lefka Mountains on the eastern side of the Samarian Gorge. The Eligias Gorge is virtually untouched. However, this trail is very difficult and a guide is a must.

Entrance to the Samaria Gorge from Aghia Roumeli (Pashley)

SELINO

KANTANOS
FLORIA
PALEOHORA

RODOVANI
ELYROS

KAMBANOS
SOUGIA - SYIA

LISSOS

PIKILASSOS

SELINO (NW HANIA)

Northwestern Chania is a fascinating district. It offers a wealth of archeological sites, natural wonders, and spectacular beaches. Kantanos, a large valley filled with olive groves, comprises most of the region. The traveler Pashley described it as a group of villages spread out on a plain whose inland border is the village of Kantanos. The trees of this olive-producing region are said to be the largest in Crete with the greatest oil output. During Venetian rule the area was a castellania and was called Selino, a name mentioned as early as 1280 when its fortress, **Castel Selino**, was built in Paleohora.

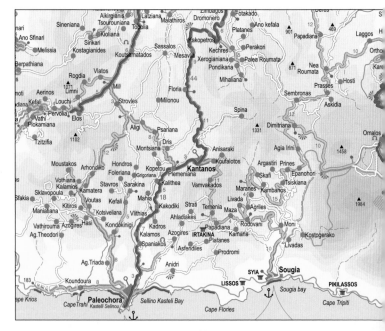

Kantanos

The town of Kantanos, the capital of the Selino province, is located at 58 kilometers along the Chania-Paleohora rural road, in a valley containing olive trees and a small river. The importance of Kantanos, whose name means "city of victory," is cited in ancient literary sources. In efforts to locate the ancient city, Pashley spoke of ruins on a hill in the southern part of the modern town. Today, scholars have established the site of ancient Kantanos to be that of the modern town and believe that it flourished during Roman times. Prior to World War II, a large building with a mosaic floor was discovered there along with parts of a statue, which according to its inscription, was dedicated to the Roman emperor Septimius Severus. During the Early Byzantine period Kantanos was a bishopric. It subsequently was destroyed by the Arabs, but was rebuilt as another bishopric during the Middle Byzantine period. This also explains the large number of Byzantine churches in the general area, most of which have frescoed interiors. During Venetian rule Kantanos was inhabited by Venetians and, likewise, was a Turkish center during Ottoman rule. In 1823 the Cretan rebels attempted to besiege the Turks but without total success. But in 1866 they finally succeed in expelling the Turks from Kantanos. The town has an illustrious history in the 20th century, as well, as the site of one of the most heroic resistance actions. The Germans retaliated by burning the entire village to the ground and putting up a sign that read: KANTANOS WAS HERE.

Byzantine Kantanos

The single-aisle church of **Mikhail Archangelos** at Kavalariana, Kantanos has a frescoed interior painted by Ioannis Pagomenos, a leading Cretan iconographer. The frescos date from 1327/28 and are distinguished for their monumental forms and perspective illusion. The 14 benefactors of the church, all members of the Kotzis family, are divided into two entities and depicted in group-portraits full of movement and vitality.

If you take the detour off the main road at Lambriana, south of Kantanos, you'll come to the church of **Aghia Kyriaki**, nestled in an

olive grove. It has one aisle and contains vestiges of frescos dating from 1402. To the right of the door is a painting of a woman and young girl dressed in white; the south wall contains the portrait of the benefactor and the name Ioannis.

Near the center of Kantanos is the reconstructed single-aisle church of **Aghia Ekaterini**, which contains traces of frescos and a beautiful stone iconostasis or altar screen.

The painted Byzantine church of Aghios Mamas ▶

Northeast of Kantanos is the settlement of Anisaraki. If you turn left at the entrance to the village and go through an olive grove you will come

Olive tree in Kantanos

to the single-aisle church of **Aghia Anna**, which contains frescoes from 1462. Worthy of note is its stone iconostasis with the Royal Doors and the two apses. The church was probably built on top of the foundations of an Early Christian basilica. The settlement of Anisaraki has three other single-aisle 14th-century churches with frescoed interiors, dedicated to the **Panaghia** (Our Lady), **Aghios Georgios**,

and **Aghia Paraskevi** respectively. The church of the Panaghia is at the exit of the village; the church of Aghia Paraskevi is located on its left and just above it.

The settlement of Plemeniana is south of Kantanos. On the right side of the road is the single-aisle church of **Sotiras Christos** (Christ the Savior). The church doesn't look old from the outside, but when you get closer you will notice that its walls contain fragments of an older Early Christian basilica.

Similar architectural fragments, which were used for structural support, are visible on the inside of the church, too. The interior also has vestiges of 14th century frescos, notable for their naïve quality. Plemeniana has another church, **Aghios Georgios**, whose frescos date from 1409/10. Portraits of the church's 5 founders are visible on the south wall.

Floria

The village of Floria is located 48 kilometers south of Chania, along the Chania-Paleohora road. It is worth visiting for its two important Byzantine churches, one in Apano (Upper) Floria and the other in Kato (Lower) Floria.

*The well-preserved church of **The Holy Fathers (Aghii Pateres)** in the Apano Floria cemetery has one aisle. Its frescos date from 1462 and are the work of the well-known artist Xenos Diyenis, who settled for a time in Crete after the fall of Constantinople in 1453.*

*In Kato Floria you can visit the church of **Aghios Georgios**. It, too, has one aisle and frescos painted by Georgios Provatopoulos in 1497. The portrait of the church's founder, Stamatis Floriotis, can be seen on the right side of the door.*

Paleohora

This town is located at the end of the Chania-Tavronitis-Paleohora rural road, 77 kilometers from Chania. Today it is a popular resort with a marvelous sand beach and excellent tourist facilities.
Nearby is the site of ancient **Kalamydi**.

Early in their rule the Venetians decided to erect a fortress on the promontory to contain rebellions in the area, which they called Castel Selino. According to Basilicata's drawing, Castel Selino, built c. 1279, had tall ramparts, towers at each corner with crenellated parapets, gates, army facilities, officers' housing, and a church. Still, the fortress proved incapable of containing the Cretan rebels who eventually captured it and razed it to the ground. The Venetians rebuilt it in 1325, only to have it destroyed again by Barbararossa and the Turks in 1653.

The beach at Paleohora

Pashley

Temenia
Yrtakina

If you take the crossroads at Kantanos and travel east for 11 kilometers you will arrive at the lush green village of Temenia, famous for its mineral water. The site of **Yrtakina**, a large city in antiquity, is located on a rocky elevation outside the village. Surviving is a segment of thick double ramparts and a temple dedicated to Pan. Pashley was the first to determine the city's position as south of Temenia and west of the ancient city of Elyros. On his visit to the rocky hill, besides the walls, he also noted a large quantity of ceramic shards. Yrtakina was a powerful city with its own coins depicting the Cretan ibex on one side and a honeybee on the other. The same coins were also used in Elyros, Tarra, and Lissos, but the Yrtakina coins also bore the inscription *YPTAKINIΩN*.

*When in Temenia you should ask to visit the Byzantine church of **Sotiras Christos** (Christ the Savior). The cruciform structure and its dome date from the 13th century, its narthex from the 14th century, and its frescos from the 16th/17th centuries.*

Rodovani – Elyros

Rodovani is 4 kilometers east of Temenia. When Pashley visited it in 1834 he noted that fragments of ancient statues had been incorporated in the village's main fountain. The village scribe sent him to **Kefali hill**, a spot with a wonderful view of the Sougia Valley and the Libyan Sea. There, he found the ruins of the city of **Elyros**: city walls, a structure with a row of arches, entablature and column fragments, and traces of an aqueduct. The structure with the arches was probably a temple dedicated to Apollo, who was worshiped in Elyros. The city continued to exist through the Roman times and was mentioned among the cities that co-signed a peace treaty

with Eumenes II of Pergamum. During Byzantine times it was a bishopric and had many churches. Some of these still survive but their frescos have been destroyed. An exception, however, is the **Church of the Panaghia** (Our Lady) at Kalomiri, which still contains the portraits of its founders, Georgios and Moschanna Kantanoleos.

The location of Elyros by Pashley

Elyros is cited in literary sources as one of the most important cities in ancient Crete. According to Stefanos Vyzantios, Elyros sent a bronze goat to Delphi to nurse Philandrus and Phylakides, the sons of Apollo and the Nymph Akakkallida. The union of Apollo and the Nymph took place in Tarra, at the house of the poet Karmanoras. Elyros developed its autonomy and ensured its self-sufficiency through farming and bee keeping. This is reflected by the fact that it had its own coins that depicted a goat on one side and a bee on the other with the inscription **ΕΛΥΡΙΩΝ.**

Kambanos

North of Rodovani is Kambanos with its abundant olive and cypress trees. The village's points of interest are its two Byzantine churches, **Aghios Polykarpos** and **Aghios Onoufrios**, which contain frescos by the well-known painter Georgios Provatopoulos.

Aghios Onoufrios

The villages of Kambanos and Tsiskiana from Rodovani

Sougia – Syia

This seaside settlement on the Libyan Sea is 70 kilometers south of Chania. Its marvelous pebble beach and sparkling water and facilities have helped make Sougia a popular tourist spot. Modern Sougia is built on top of the ruins of **Syia**, the ancient port of Elyros. Its name comes from the ancient Greek word "sys," meaning pig, so one can assume that this was once a forested area where pigs were bred. Literary sources refer to Syia as a small city, but having a very good harbor. The ruins of buildings, graves, and cisterns attest to its prosperity during Greco-Roman times. It flourished, too, during the Early Christian period, as seen by the remains of **three Early Christian basilicas** with mosaic decoration. One of these was discovered west of the village in 1953. Measuring 20.8 X 12.40 meters, it had three aisles with a narthex and mosaics dating from the 6th century AD. The other two basilicas were found on the east side of the bay. Of these only one had a mosaic floor.

Lissos

This small coastal ancient city west of Syia was built in a well-protected bay. You can visit Lissos by taking the trail at the western end of the Syia bay. Lissos is an hour's walk away. The ruins here were first identified as

The Asclepiion in Lissos

the ancient city of Lissos in 1834 by the traveler Robert Pashley, who managed to reach even this remote place. During antiquity its inhabitants were evidently engaged

The pebble beach at Sougia

in fishing and trade, and the city was so wealthy that it minted its own gold coins and was known as far away as the north coast of Africa. The city's coins bear the head of Artemis on one side and a dolphin on the other with the inscription ΛΙΣΙΩΝ. It flourished particularly during Hellenistic and Roman times and owed much of its reputation to its mineral spring, which also explains the existence of an **Asclepiion**, or temple dedicated to Asclepius, the Greek god of medicine. Votive statues, figurines and inscriptions dedicated to Asclepius and the goddess Hygeia (the Health Giver) have been found inside the Doric sanctuary. The temple building dates from the 4th century BC; its mosaic floor was added in the 1st century BC. Archeologists have discovered harbor facilities, private dwellings, and graves at the site, and by Pashley's accounts there was also a theater.

Lissos continued to exist into Early Christian times, as witnessed by the remains of Early Christian basilicas beneath the modern churches of the **Panaghia** and **Aghios Kyrkos** or Kyriakos. In fact, architectural fragments from an earlier basilica are visible in Aghios Kyrkos.

Pikilassos

This ancient city, located between Syia (Sougia) and Tarra (Aghia Roumeli), was built on the Trypiti promontory. It was inhabited in Hellenistic times, but abandoned during Roman times, and probably served as a port for Elyros. Archeologists have discovered the ruins of two temples there.

The route from Sougia to Lissos is very exciting. First it goes through a small ravine and then ascends into the mountains. All at once at the highest point you see the Bay of Lissos, the steep mountains, and the Libyan Sea opening before you. From there the road descends, taking you to the ancient city that served as the harbor of Yrtakina.

COLFO E SPIAGGIE D' CHISSAMO

KISSAMOS (NORTHWESTERN HANIA)

Kissamos, the northwestern portion of the Chania prefecture, is mostly mountainous. It does, however, have some large relatively flat expanses that are filled with countless olive trees.

This region at Crete's westernmost tip is famous for its fantastic sandy beaches, green landscape, beautiful ravines, picturesque villages, and unique archeological sites.

Kolymbari Gonia Monastery

Located 23 kilometers west of Chania inside the large bay, Kolymbari is known for its olive oil and wine.

It was here that the Turks landed in 1645, before going on to capture Chania and the rest of Crete. Just outside Kolymbari is

The olive tree of Kolymbari, the largest of its kind in Crete

Tradition has it that **Gonia Monastery** was founded in the 9th century, but not in its present location. Initially it was in Menies, on the northern tip of the Spatha promontory, where once there had been a sanctuary to Artemis. But since this spot was vulnerable to pirate raids, in the 17th century the monastery moved further south to where it is today. It is said, moreover, that the move was prompted by a vision had by the monk Vlassios. Its reconstruction began in 1618 and was completed in 1634. When the Turks landed in this region in 1645 the monastery was completely destroyed. It was rebuilt in 1651 as Stauropigean monastery, namely it fell under the jurisdiction of Constantinople Patriarchate, and had a school on its premises. The next catastrophe in the revolution of 1821 was not its last. Two others followed before the monastery was to see the light of Cretan independence, when, in 1861, it became headquarters for the first Greek army on the island.

the Gonia Monastery that is dedicated to the Virgin Mary (Panaghia). When Pashley visited it in 1834 he wrote that it was built on an elevation right on the coast and that its church contained many icons that had been sent to Trieste for safekeeping when the revolution broke out. He also reported that the monastery was very wealthy with a lot of land and monks. It is

Ritzos.

Near Gonia Monastery is the Orthodox Academy of Crete, a center of scientific and intellectual activities.

Scattered remains of the Sanctuary of Diktynna

Diktynna

In the bay of Menies, Rodopos on the northeastern point of the Spatha promontory - known as Tityros or Psakkon in antiquity - are the ruins of what once was the splendid Roman sanctuary of

Diktynna. This place where the Cretan goddess Diktynna was worshipped was a major cult center whose income went to the construction of public works. Diktynna is identified with Artemis Britomartis

built like a fortress with the *katholikon* or main church in the center of an inner courtyard. The structure around the perimeter houses the abbot's quarters, monks' cells, refectory, and auxiliary rooms. The cathedral has a narthex, two chapels, and a dome. The monastery's museum contains artifacts, manuscripts, vestments, and icons from the 15th, 16th and 17th centuries. Several of the icons are by the famous painter of the Cretan School, Andreas

*In Christian times (9th century), the church of **Aghios Georgios** was built here in the place that would eventually become Gonia Monastery. Because it was vulnerable to pirate attacks, the location was abandoned and the monastery was rebuilt further south. The church of Aghios Georgios and the remains of the monastery still survive, 3 kilometers from Menies.*

(or the sweet virgin), the offspring of the Minoan goddess of nature and fertility. Since Pashley considered that the location of the ancient city of Diktynneo had already been established, he did not feel a visit to it was necessary. The traveler Pococke, in his "Description of the Orient" (1743-1745), mentions the remains of structures built of gray marble and talks about a building resembling a church, cisterns, and what were probably the ruins of a temple. According to literary testimony, dogs guarded the sanctuary because of the great wealth of offerings it contained. Excavations carried out by the Germans during the Second World War proved the existence of a large temple in the center of a courtyard surrounded by stoae. Fragments of this temple have survived. To its west one can see remains of the Roman aqueduct created to serve the sanctuary's needs. Diktynna has only a chapel and a fantastic sandy beach. You can reach it by land or by boat from Chania.

The Bay of Menies

Episkopi

The village of Episkopi is 32 kilometers from Chania. To get there you take the national road from Chania towards Kastelli and turn south at the Kolymbari intersection. As its name implies, Episkopi was the bishop's see during the Middle Byzantine and early Venetian periods (from 961 AD to the arrival of the Venetians).

*The episcopal church, better known as the **Rotonda**, was dedicated to the **Archangel Michael**, and as Gerola writes, its architectural design is unlike any on Crete. The main part of the church is divided into three horizontal sections: 1. the narthex; 2. The middle portion that contains the central circular section topped by a stepped dome and two smaller ones left and right; 3. The three eastern segments containing the central apse, the prothesis or offertory, and the diaconicon or sacristy. On the west, north and south sides of the episcopal church are buildings that communicate with the main church and a very likely part of the bishop's mansion or extensions of the church structure. Preserved inside the church is a portion of the mosaic floor, a marble baptismal font, and frescos from a number of periods.*

Astrikas

In 1933, two **chamber tombs** from the 8th century BC were discovered in the village of Astrikas, 3 kilometers outside of Episkopi further south. One of them is considered to be the richest geometric-period tomb excavated to date. It was filled with gold, bronze, and clay grave offerings, now on exhibit in the Archeological Museum of Chania.

Nopigeia – Rokka

Nopigeia

Voukolies

Voukolies (26.5 kilometers southwest of Chania) is reached by following the Chania-Tavronitis-Paleohora route. If you turn left at the entrance to the village and proceed 500 meters you come to the church of **Aghios Konstantinos**. This well-preserved, small single-aisle church contains portions of frescos dating from 1452 and 1462.

Nopigeia is a seaside settlement 36 kilometers west of Chania. Pashley, who incorrectly called the area Nopia, visited some ancient ruins near the church of Aghios Georgios, west of the village. He reported that the church had a north-south orientation – a deviation from the ecclesiastical norm - and was built on the foundations of an ancient temple. He believed that these ruins were part of the ancient city of **Mithymna**. In 1983, excavations on Trouli

Hill revealed an early Minoan settlement wit continuous habitation into Classical and Roman times, except for a brief interruption, desertion during the 12th century BC. Roma ruins including an aqueduct and baths ca be seen there today. Mithymna is believed to have been the port of an inland city that was probably situated where the village of Rokka is today. There are traces of a Byzantine fortress on Rokka's craggy Trouli Hill and chisel marks in the rock identified as 3rd/2nd century BC housing foundations.

Trouli Hill

Villa Trevisan

*The settlement of **Kokkino Metohi** is located in the village of **Drapanias**, 36.5 kilometers west of Chania on the old national Chania-Kastelli road. It is worth visiting for its Venetian-era Villa Trevisan, one of the best examples of Venetian-period country residences with clear Renaissance-style architectural details, particularly on the second story. Over the entrance are pedimental lintels with the Trevisan family crest and the windows have ornamental protruding supports. The building has two stories with an exterior staircase supported by arches.*

Voulgaro - Latziana - Topolia

Take the Chania-Kastelli national road and turn left at Nopigeia onto the rural road that takes you south/southeast to Elafonissi. After 7 kilometers, at the exit to Voulgaro, you turn left again onto the narrow road leading to the settlement of **Latziana**. There in the gully next to a natural spring is a modern church. Just below it are the ruins of the large church of **Aghia Varvara** (Saint Barbara), which served as the **katholikon** or main church of a convent and dates from the second half of the 11th century. The structure was cruciform

with a dome. The ancient architectural fragments you see scattered around the site and incorporated into the walls are segments of the four Roman columns used to support the church's dome. The church's painted decoration includes saints in frontal poses and scenes from the life of Christ. Some of the frescos are still in situ; others have been removed and are on exhibit in the Chania Byzantine and Post-Byzantine Collection. North of Latziana is the settlement of **Mouri**. The dirt road leads to the north side of a hill that is topped with the church of **Aghios Antonios**. While you're in the area, it's worth taking this road south to

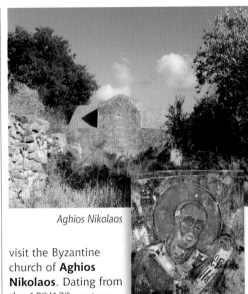

Aghios Nikolaos

visit the Byzantine church of **Aghios Nikolaos**. Dating from the 12th/13th century, the church has an architectural form that is particularly rare in Crete: a cruciform whose central nave is higher than the two side aisles. The church interior was covered with frescos, most impressive of which is the monumental linear, schematic rendering of Saint Nicholas.

If you continue on the rural road you will come to the village of **Topolia,** 9 kilometers south of Voulgaro. Built like an amphitheater in a lush green valley, Topolia is a large, wealthy village with considerable holiday conveniences. The 1500-meter-long Topolian Gorge starts from here. It has rich

Aghios Antonios must be seen for its panorama of the northern coastline and surrounding villages with ancient Polyrrinia in the distance.

flora and tall, vertical walls that reach 300 meters at certain points. You can go through the gorge by car since the road runs along its west side. A tunnel has even been opened in one place. On the right side of the road at the gorge's exit you will see the **cave of Aghia Sofia** and the little church of the same name.

Kalathenes

A small detour 3 kilometers west of Topolia takes you to the village of Kalathenes (50 kilometers from Chania). Visitors come here mostly for the Venetian structure known as the **rotunda**. The building was the villa of a Venetian lord and dates from the 15th/16th century. Although inspired by Renaissance models, it has its own unique architectural character.

Chrysoskalitissa – Elafonissi

The convent of Chrysoskalitissa (71 kilometers from Chania and 38 kilometers from Kastelli) is built on a sheer cliff overlooking the sea on the west coast of Crete. Dedicated to the Assumption of the Virgin Mary, legend has it that the convent is called Chrysoskalitissa (Golden Staircase) because one of the 90 steps leading to the top of the cliff is made of gold. The convent probably existed during Venetian rule but the facts we have are scant. What is certain, however, is that it did not operate during the Turkish occupation that lasted into the mid-19th century. A few nuns remain and the convent provides shelter for fishermen and sailors when the weather gets rough.

Chrysoskalitissa

The memorial to Elafonissi in the roots of a cedar tree

It's worth a visit for the spectacular view.
6 kilometers south is the famous **Elafonissi** (= "slightly" an island), which as its name declares is a small island virtually connected to the coast of Crete. It is just 100 meters off shore and you reach it by walking through the water. Elafonissi is 76 kilometers from Chania and 43 from Kastelli.

People come here to admire the spectacular beaches, sand dunes, and white sand and to swim in the crystal clear turquoise water found nowhere else on Crete. Although its natural beauty attracts innumerable visitors, the area does not offer many tourist amenities.
The history of Elafonissi is associated with a tragedy that took place in 1824. At the time 850 people had gathered there to escape from Ibrahim Pasha who had destroyed the entire island. Unfortunately, the Turks found them out and slaughtered them, turning the sea red with blood.
If you take the dirt road west along the coast you will come to the **Cedar Forest**, with its bay and sandy beach of the same name.

Cedar Forest

Elafonissi

Inahorion

The area of southwestern Crete that is bordered on the south by Elafonissi, on the north by Sfinari, and on the east by the villages of Aligi and Mylones is known as Inahorion. Also spelled with a double N, Inahorion or Ennea Horia (Nine Villages) offers both natural and cultural interest. What may be the most picturesque villages in Crete cling to the steep green slopes facing the island's western coast. Fascinating forested footpaths take you to traditional villages, most of which have been completely restored, and Byzantine churches. Of special note is the beautiful village of **Kefali**, with its painted Byzantine church of the Transformation of Christ

According to one opinion, the name **Inahorion** signifies the nine villages, but in actuality there are 16. There is also another theory that the name In(n)ahorion has no connection to the number nine, and that the modern name "Ennea Horia" (Nine Villages) is a corruption of the original "Ina horion." Either way, according to Ptolemy, there was a city in Roman Crete called Inahorion, and based on archeological evidence it must have been situated near the villages of Perivolia and Kouneni (now Vathi).

Vathi, Aghios Georgios

(**Metamorphosis tou Sotira**) and spectacular view. The village of **Vathi**, once called Kouneni, has many Byzantine churches. Don't miss the single-aisle, frescoed church of **Aghios Georgios** (1284) inside the village, and the church of **Aghios Ioannis**

The village of Kefali

Chrysostomos (St. John the Chrysostom). Vathi also contains the church of **Mikhail Archangelos** with its well-preserved 14th

Leaving Papadiana

Vathi, Aghios Ioannis

century frescos, and the little Catholic Church of **Santa Maria**. Nearby are the picturesque villages of **Simantiriana,** **Papadiana**, and **Amygdalokefali** with a wonderful view of the west coast.

Falassarna

The archeological site of Falassarna is located on the west coast of Crete, at the base of the Gramvoussa promontory, in a large, fertile plain. Based on excavation evidence, the city, which is named after the Nymph Falassarni, must have been founded c. 6th century BC. But judging from the establishment of the other large cities in western Crete, it is quite possible that Falassarna was founded as early as the 8th century BC. As a coastal city, which was also the port of Polyrrinia, Falassarna

The "Throne"

developed into an important naval and commercial power, famous for its harbor that was enclosed by walls. The elevation of coastline on western Crete turned both the harbor and the canal connecting it to the sea into grassland. Pashley, who visited the remains of the ancient city in 1834, observed a group of some thirty tombs

The harbor's circular fortification tower. 4th century BC

of the harbor's four fortification towers, which date from the 4th century BC. Being an independent and autonomous city, Falassarna, also known as Falassarni, minted its own coins, which had the head of a woman with earrings on one side and a trident and the inscription ΦA on

the other. In addition to the archeological site, the area has an enormous sandy beach and tourist facilities, making it an increasingly popular vacation spot on the island.

The beach at Falassarna

carved into the rock on the southwestern side and an enormous stone seat. He believed the seat to be a kind of throne to hold a statue of the honored god, who in this case might have been Poseidon since it is a coastal city, or Diktynna who had a temple in her honor in Falassarna. There is another theory that this throne, rather than being a seat, was simply a speaker's "rostrum." Pashley also noted the well-preserved remains of the walls with towers in the northern section. Today, besides the temple, the tombs, and the throne, you can see sections of the walls as well as two (one circular, the other square)

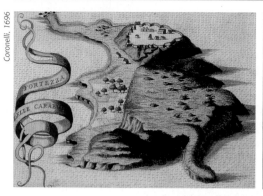

Coronelli, 1696

Korykon. Ptolemy called both the promontory and the city Korykos, and Pliny called the two islets Korikiae. No one is certain whether a city named Korykos ever existed, but the place on the promontory now known as Aghios

Imeri Gramvoussa

Gramvoussa

Gramvoussa is the name of Crete's northwest peninsula of Crete. The tiny islands in front of it are called **Imeri (Cultivated) Gramvoussa and Agria (Wild) Gramvoussa**. Gramvoussa promontory, known

as Tigani today, was called **Kimaros** by the ancient geographer Strabo and by other geographers as

Sostis was definitely the site of the Roman city **Agneion**. The Venetians designated the promontory as

*The highest point of the steepest cliff was chosen as the site of the **fortress**. Its ramparts were fortified with bastions on all sides except for those whose cliffs were so tall and steep that they provided their own natural protection. The fort, whose main entrance was on its east side, contained all the necessary facilities such as ammunition depots, cisterns, barracks, and a church dedicated to the Annunciation. Because of its position and its strong ramparts the fortress was considered unassailable. In fact, the Venetians managed to hold on to it, together with Suda and Spinalonga, until 1682, long after the Turks had overtaken the rest of Crete. It played a vital role as a rebel refuge during the Greek rebellion of 1821. Isolation, however, forced the rebels to take up piracy. So the Anglo-French fleet captured the island in 1828 and appointed an English garrison commander. With the London protocol of 1830 Gramvoussa passed once again into Turkish hands.*

Capo Buso on their maps, and Gramvoussa is probably a corruption of that name. The two little islands also take their names from there: the northernmost is Agria Gramvoussa and the other one is Imeri Gramvoussa, which is also called Aghios Nikolaos after the little church it contains. Since the little harbor of Imeri Gramvoussa was the first port of Crete encountered by inbound ships from Adriatica, the Venetians decided to fortify it. In fact,

Basilica reports that this harbor was the most important bastion in the Kingdom of Crete. The reconstruction of the fortress began in 1583 and continued at such a rapid pace that it was completed by 1584. It has survived in excellent condition and you can visit it by boat from Kastelli, Kissamos.

FORT.^e DE LA GARABVSA.   A. MAGASINO DE LA PROVISIONE, U.
B. LA MVNITIONE.   C. CASA DE PROVED.
D. LA PORTA.

The trip takes about an hour and is well worth it not only for the fort but also for the opportunity to swim there and at

Balos from the fortress

Balos, the beach on the peninsula just across the way. You can reach the sandy beach of Balos with its turquoise water overland by the dirt road from the village of Kalyviani, just east of Falassarna. The road ends 2 kilometers from the beach and you have to walk the rest of the way.

Balos

Kastelli or Kissamos

Kastelli Kissamou or Kissamos is a seaside town on the gulf of the same name, 42 kilometers west of Chania. The fertile plain, favorable to the production of olives, grapes, and citrus fruits, has made the region quite wealthy. Although it offers the amenities, it does not get very many tourists. Whatever tourism the area does have is due to the ferry service between Kastelli and the Peloponnese (mainland Greece). Kissamos was recorded by Pliny and by Ptolemy as a flourishing city in Roman times from the 1st century BC to the 4th century AD. It was built on the site of

a prehistoric settlement and served as the port for Polyrrinia. It was autonomous and had its own coins that depicted Hermes, symbolizing the city's commerce activity. Literary sources tell us that Kissamos had

an aqueduct during Roman times, as well as a theater and other important buildings. Furthermore, current excavations continue to uncover sumptuous homes with mosaic floors, baths, and underground tombs.

*Basilicata sketched in detail views of the **Bay of Kissamos** set between the two promontories of Cavo Spada and Cavo Buso, and the fertile valley with its rivers and settlements. He also rendered many monasteries and churches, as well as the then surviving fragments of the walls of the **castle** built by the Genoese architect Enrico Pescatore. The castle was built on top of the ruins of an ancient city. In the 13th century it passed into the hands of the Venetians, who utilized it to quell Cretan uprisings. It was destroyed numerous times and rebuilt by the Venetians themselves, who frequently incorporated the ancient architectural elements that they found scattered around the area. The Turks then arrived on the island and, in 1646, the castle passed into their hands. Except for some sections of the ramparts, virtually nothing survives of the castle today.*

Polyrrinia

6 kilometers south of Kastelli Kissamou is the archeological site of ancient Polyrrinia and the modern village of the same name, once known as Paleokastro. The village was built on top of the ancient city. Many ancient architectural elements were used in construction and are clearly visible in the walls of the buildings. The entire region, and especially the citadel, contains remains from every period that the city was occupied from antiquity to Byzantine times. These ruins include the **walls**, which impressed Pashley enough to draw them. One of the most interesting is the Roman **aqueduct**, a work of the Hadrianic era (117-138 AD).

Polyrrinia was one of the most powerful cities in ancient Crete and certainly the second most powerful in western Crete, after Kydonia. It was built on a naturally fortified site with a limitless view of the entire area from the Sea of Crete to the Libyan Sea. Although the modern village was built on top of the antiquities, thereby limiting archeological excavation and findings, there is no doubt of the city's existence by Minoan times. Strabo corroborates this view, testifying that the inhabitants of Polyrrinia originally lived in separate settlements or small districts that the Achaians and Lakedaimonians then united into a single powerful city. Polyrrinia means a place with many sheep, and the name confirms that its inhabitants were primarily involved in animal raising.

There is also the **church of the Holy Fathers (Agii Pateres)** on the citadel, which is built almost exclusively from architectural fragments of ancient temples. Its walls hold inscriptions containing valuable information about the city. Of particular interest is the inscription dating from 69 BC referring to the Roman conqueror of Crete, Quinctius Caecilius

Metellus, as the savior and benefactor of the city. In other words, Polyrrinia did not participate with the other cities

of Crete in resisting the Roman conquest, perhaps because of its history of hostility with Kydonia and Knossos. Thus Polyrrinia flourished in Roman times. Literary sources tell us that the citadel contained a **temple of Diktynnis Artemis** and that the Polyrrinians also worshiped Zeus and Athena. As a powerful and independent city, it had its own coins, most of which have the crowned head of Zeus on the front and the head of a bull with the inscription ΠΟΛΥΡΡΗΝΙΟΝ on the reverse.

GAVDOS

The island of Gavdos is the southernmost island not only of Crete but also of all Europe. It is 32 nautical miles from Paleohora and 26 from Hora Sfakion. It is triangular shaped and has a total surface area of 29.60 square kilometers, a warm, dry climate, and little rainfall. As a result the island has a serious water shortage. Among the natural beauties of

Potamos

Gavdos are its pine and cedar trees, and of course the wonderful pristine beaches and sparkling seas at Sarakino, Korfos, and Potamos. The island has only a handful of full-time residents. Boats run between the coastal settlements of Paleohora and Hora Sfakion on the Cretan

Lighthouse

mainland, but frequent, powerful winds prevent them from maintaining a regular schedule. Tourist amenities on

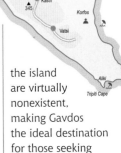

the island are virtually nonexistent, making Gavdos the ideal destination for those seeking peace and relaxation. After a 2-3 hour voyage you arrive in the little harbor of Karave, which has several taverns and a few rooms to let. The capital, Kastri, 5 kilometers away, offers the basic public services. The island's landmark is the **Faros or Lighthouse** on the road to Ambelos, built in 1880 by the French Ottoman Lighthouse Company.

Depiction of a Roman Empire farmstead with an olive press

first settled in the Neolithic era and continued to be inhabited through Christian times. Called **Kavdos** in historical times, it came under the influence of the powerful city of Gortyn. This is documented in a 3rd century BC

Cedar tree

inscription that speaks of a pact between the two cities whereby the islanders would retain their liberty on the island but were obligated to

pay produce taxes to Gortyn (i.e. on salt and cedar cones), and back it in its wars. In addition to the valued cedar cones, which are thought to promote fertility, Gavdos produces wheat and excellent quality lamb and goat meat.

During the Roman era the island was also known as **Clavdi**, perhaps in honor of Claudius Caesar, and in Byzantine times as the Island of **Klavdos**, the seat of the bishopric. The Venetians called it **Gozzo** and the Turks **Bugadoz**.

Unfortunately, the lighthouse was bombed in World War II and only its ruins survive today.

The ancient Greek poet and scholar Callimachus identified Gavdos as the mythical **Ogygia**, which according to the Odyssey of Homer was the island of the nymph Calypso. Archeological excavations confirm that Gavdos was

Gavdopoula

ROUTES

HANIA - SOUGIA - LISSOS

You leave Chania by the national highway and follow the road to Omalos. This is one of the four main arteries crossing the prefecture of Chania from north to south. After 3 kilometers there is a road on the left to *Potistiria*, 500 meters past you see a road on the right to *Galatas*, and after another 500 meters a road on the left to *Marmara*. You travel another 500 meters and arrive at the left turn leading to *Varypetro* (2 km). Another 1.5 kilometers brings you to the left turn for *Myloniana* (2 km). You head southwards and after 1 kilometer you reach an intersection on the right to *Kyrtomado*

(2 km) and **Aghia Lake**. It's worth taking a detour and visiting this artificial lake, one of the two lakes on Crete. Its important wetlands are home to rare birds and rich plant life during the spring. You then return to the

main road to Omalos. After 2 kilometers you reach the turn for Omalos (26 km), Skines (4 km), Sougia (54 km), and Alikianos (1 km). At this junction you will find an informative map of the Municipality of Mousouri with many routes to the Lefka Mountains and the Samarian Gorge. Turn right towards **Alikianos** and cross the old stone bridge over the Keritis River. Alikianos is a large village known for its orange groves and distinctive aristocratic homes. After Alikianos you turn right towards Vatolakkos and the Church of Zoodohou Pighis. While in the village, take the first intersection towards Koufos, which takes you to the *Byzantine church of Aghios Georgios*, also inside the village. Park your car near the church and walk through the gardens to the *Villa Da Molin*. Nestled among orange trees and choked by ivy, only portions of the Villa's walls survive

in derelict condition. You again take the main road through the village and turn right at the first road just past Aghios Georgios. After 1 kilometer you reach the reconstructed frescoed church of *Zoodohou Pighi or Ai Kyr Yannis* (You can also visit the church by taking the road on the right at the exit of the village). You return to Alikianos and then follow the road south for 1 kilometer to **Vatolakkos**. Vatolakkos has an impressive central square with a large church and bell tower, as well as a marvelous view of the area's orange groves. After returning to Alikianos you exit the

village and turn right on to the rural road to Sougia. Two kilometers later you arrive at the village of **Skines**, and 2 kilometers after that the village of **Khliaro**. At the exit of this little village there is a large intersection on the left to Karanos (9 km) and Orthouni (5 km). You continue driving south towards Sougia. You have already reached the northwest foot of the Lefka Mountains. The orange groves have given way to a hillier landscape filled with olive and chestnut trees.

CHESTNUT TREES

AGHIA IRINI

2 kilometers further south is the village of **Langos**, built in the ravine (=langadia) from which it obviously gets its name. From here the road narrows and has many bends. 4 kilometers past Langos is a private park where you can rest and have a drink at the natural spring. The road continues to climb along the northwestern slopes of the Lefka Mountains, winding its way through a terrain of shrubbery. Immediately after this, you pass by an intersection on the left to the village of Hosti (5 km) and come upon a valley filled with olive trees, plane trees, chestnut trees and arbutus. The village of Nea Roumata can be seen in the distance. Just before you reach the village you will see a road on the

PRASSES

right with a sign leading to an Early Minoan tholos tomb. It's worth making the 500-meter detour to visit this stone tomb containing a skeleton in a crouched position and two pots. Once again

on the main road, the village of **Nea Roumata** is 2.5 kilometers away (a total of 26 kilometers from Chania). Inside the village is the crossroads for *Papadiana* (5 km) and *Deres* (7 km). Follow the sign to Sougia (41 kilometers). 3 kilometers later (29 kilometers on the national road) there is a place where you can pull over and admire a panoramic view. The drive to the village of Prasses is spectacular, offering unforgettable views of

the western foothills of the cypress covered Lefka Mountains that you approach through area forested with chestnut trees. At the 31st kilometer you come to **Prasses**. Here in the village square you can relax in one of the many cafes and enjoy the view of the Lefka Mountains. Chestnut trees are everywhere and if you visit in the fall you will have the unique pleasure of both seeing as well as tasting the fresh chestnuts. 4 kilometers later is a right turn-off to the village of *Sembronas* (2 km). Instead of turning, you continue the ascent through a terrain that is now entirely alpine

and filled with shrubs. 4 kilometers further south (at the 39th kilometer) is a left turn that takes you to the Omalos plateau. This is the highest point of the route and offers a panorama of the Libyan Sea, the Aghia Irini Gorge, and the Lefka Mountains. As you descend, you see before you a lush green valley and the imposing entrance to the Aghia Irini Gorge. 3 kilometers later (42nd kilometer) you reach the small village of **Aghia Irini** nestled in the valley. Continuing on, 3 kilometers south (45th kilometer) you see the impressive entrance to the Aghia Irini Gorge to your left. At this point you should get off the car and walk to the gorge. The landscape is alpine and filled with cypress trees. Just after you enter the gorge you can stop at a lovely park and refreshment stand where hikers can purchase provisions for the trail ahead. After going through the gorge you return to the main road. Just beyond this point (45th kilometer) you will pass **Epanohori** and see the Libyan Sea before you. After also passing the village of **Prines** (46th kilometer) and the right-hand turn at the 47th kilometer leading to *Argastiri* (5 km) and **Tsiskiana**, you arrive at the village of **Kambanos** (51st kilometer). There you will find the 15th century church of Aghios Onoufrios containing frescos by the painter Provatopoulos. Outside the village is a crossroads that goes right to Skafi (1 kilometer) and straight ahead to Paleohora (27 km) and Sougia (15 km). Continue in the direction of Sougia past the villages of **Maralia** and **Agriles**, which are built on a slope facing a beautiful valley. 4 kilometers beyond Kambanos (55th kilometer point) is a crossroads leading right to Rodovani (1) and Paleohora (22 km), and left to Sougia (11 km). After 50 meters on the road to Sougia you will see a sign pointing to **Ancient Elyros**. Take a detour on the road, which is paved only at the beginning, and follow the dirt road 1 kilometer up Kefalas Hill. There is a great view of the Lefka

KEFALA

Mountains on the west and the Libyan Sea on the south. Aside from the ruins of the ancient city, Kefalas Hill also has a modern church dedicated to the Panaghia built on

AGHIOS NIKOLAOS

top of a Byzantine church whose remains are clearly visible. Back on the central road, 5 kilometers in the direction of Sougia you turn left on an asphalt road marked with a sign to the restored church of Aghios Nikolaos. After this detour you return to the central road and soon

AG. IRINI - GORGE

arrive at the village of **Moni** (61 kilometers). The road through the village parallels the riverbank and the exit of the Aghia Irini Gorge. 3 kilometers south is the left turn leading to *Koustoyerako* (7 km) and *Leivadas* (4 km). Follow this for 1 kilometer and then take another left turn to the exit of Aghia Irini Gorge, where there is a lovely park and a refreshment stand built of stone. You return to the road to **Koustoyerako,** which you will reach after 7 kilometers of steep upgrade. Besides being uphill, this stretch of road is filled with curves. It rewards us, however, with the panorama of the valley and the exit to the gorge. At the

KOUSTOYERAKO

entrance to the village there is a monument to the National Resistance and an ideal place to stop and admire the unique view of the Libyan Sea and the valley. After visiting Koustoyerako you return to the main road to Sougia. You follow the riverbank for 4 kilometers (70th kilometer) and arrive in **Sougia**. At the west end of the pebble beach is the entrance to the E4 trail that leads to the bay and the ancient site of **Lissos**. The hike takes 1 hour and 15 minutes but is well worth the effort. You go through a small ravine and up through a pine forest to suddenly arrive at a plateau from which you see the bay and the archeological site on the beach.

HANIA – PALEOHORA

You leave Chania on the national road going west towards Kastelli. After passing the crossroads for Platanias, you turn right at the 19th kilometer point towards *Paleohora* (51 km). You drive through the village of **Neratzia** (24 km), and after 2 kilometers you arrive in **Voukolies** (26 km), a large village with schools, public services, and tourist facilities.

At the entrance to the village, take the detour to the left onto a small paved road marked to the church of *Aghios Konstantinos*. As the sign tells us, the church is 500 meters away. After the first few meters the paved road turns to dirt and takes you to the orange grove where the church is located. The single-aisle church, which is well preserved, has a noteworthy bell tower and lintel. It was

VOUKOLIES

AGHIOS KONSTANTINOS

evidently completely painted but only portions of the frescos survive. The terrain is mostly flat with olive trees and citrus orchards as well as cypress and plane trees. You return to the main road and make a left turn going south to Paleohora. At the exit of the village there is a monument to the fallen in the revolt of 1897 on your left-hand side. A bit further

down to the right there is a fork in the road. One fork goes west to *Glossa* (2 km) and *Koumares* (1 km), and the other, which is unmarked, is the dirt road going northwest to Hadjitraganos Metohi. You leave the main road to go to Koumares. Here you come upon

GLOSSA

a spectacular sight: an enormous plane of olive trees and the outline of northern Crete with the peninsulas of Gramvoussa and Rodopos. After 1 kilometer you come to the village of **Koumares**, and after 2 kilometers **Glossa**, which deserves a visit if you want a taste of authentic Cretan village life. Drive back the same way you came and then take the second fork to Hadjitraganos Metohi. On the left of this rural dirt track is a panorama of the Kolymbari olive orchard and the Rodopos promontory and a clear view of the villages of Koumares and Glossa.

After 1 kilometer you make a left-hand turn onto a narrower rural road that gets to the reconstructed single-aisle church of *Aghios Vassilios* at **Hadjitraganos Metohi** after some 500 meters. After this most

AGHIOS VASSILIOS

interesting detour, which we highly recommend (total distance 10 kilometers), you return to the original fork in the road and resume your main route. Just down the road is a crossroads that goes left to Anoskeli and straight ahead to Paleohora (45 km). Continue going straight. 4 kilometers later you reach the village of **Dromonero** where there is a right turn to Kolymbari (16 km). This road, which is not on your route, goes through the olive grove and is only for the adventurous. The village center of **Kakopetros**, 4 kilometers down the road, has an intersection

going left to Palea Roumata (4 km). You continue in the direction of Paleohora, stopping on the right after 3 kilometers to admire the spectacular view of the entire Bay of Kissamos and the peninsulas of Gramvoussa and Rodopos. 2 kilometers further south is the village of Mesavlia (40th kilometer). Once in the village, take the right turn with the sign marked Aghia Paraskevi and the Mesavliano Gorge. The Gorge

deserves a visit for its marvelous vegetation and wide variety of trees from plane and chestnut trees to olive and citrus. If you descend into Mesavliano Gorge you then can take the dirt

road to Malathiro where there was a Byzantine castle. You return to the main road and after 4 kilometers (45th) you come to the village of **Floria**. Inside the village make a right turn for Sassalo (7 kilometers). 1 kilometer from here is the painted single-aisle church of *Aghios Georgios*. Return to the main road and turn right again inside the village and then left on to the small asphalt road. Leave your car after 1 kilometer and follow the dirt road on the right on foot down to the church of the *Aghii Pateres* (Holy Fathers). This little church, with some vestiges of frescos, is situated in a lush ravine that is worth seeing for its natural beauty. You return to the village and turn left on the main

road towards Paleohora. After 20 kilometers, at the 60th kilometer point, you arrive in **Kantanos**. Once at the entrance, follow the sign on the right to the Byzantine church of *Aghios Mamas*, and then return to the town center. Kantanos, in fact, is a large town with a municipal hall, public

services, banks, shops, and tourist facilities. In and around the town are many Byzantine churches that are worth visiting for their exceptional frescos. Follow the dirt roads marked to *Aghia Kyriaki* at Lambriana. This single-aisle church has vestiges of fresco decoration dating from 1402. Return again to the village center. North of the high school is a small road leading to the famous church of *Mikhail Archangelos* at Kavalariana. This single-aisle church is decorated with frescos by the renowned painter Ioannis Pagomenos and dates from 1327/28. From the center of the village you take the road to Temenia and Sougia. When you come to the settlement called

Anisaraki, follow the sign to the church of *Aghia Anna*. You walk through an olive grove to reach the single-aisle church with its stone iconostasis and frescos from the 14th century. After this brief tour of the major churches of Kantanos, you return to the village center and proceed towards Paleohora. 1 kilometer later (61st) you arrive at **Plemeniana**. Turn right and follow the sign to the church of *Sotiras Christos*. Apart from its 14th century fresco fragments, this church is particularly interesting because it was built incorporating architectural elements from an Early Christian basilica. Continue south, past the villages of **Kakodiki, Vlithias** and **Spaniakos**. Vlithias contains the Byzantine church of

the Metamorphosis (Transfiguration) with frescos from 1359. Spaniakos also has several painted Byzantine churches (Panaghia, Aghios Georgios and Aghia Marina). 17 kilometers later you reach **Paleohora**, a total of 77 kilometers from Chania. In this seaside town you can enjoy a swim at the

beautiful, full-facility sandy beach and visit the fortress Castel Selino. You return to Chania on the same road that you took to get there. In **Dromonero** at the 38th kilometer point turn left towards Kolymbari. This is the entrance to the Mesavliano Gorge, which you visited on your way to Paleohora. This route takes you through a fascinating landscape of olive trees and picturesque villages such as **Metohi** and **Aghios Antonios**. The latter has an attractive outdoor theater of stone named after the famous Greek actor Alexis Minotis. After driving 9 kilometers through a green valley you come to a crossroads where there is a left turn to Deliana and the Deliana Gorge (7 kilometers). You will continue right, however, and arrive at the village of **Episkopi**. (You can also reach this village by

the Chania-Kolymbari-Episkopi route, 32 kilometers.) Follow the signs to the *rotunda*, the *episcopal church of Mikhail Archangelos*, the bishopric with its unique architecture, stepped dome, and frescos. You then leave Episkopi and 4 kilometers past it you reach **Spilia** to the north. Turn left in the village towards Aghios Ioannis the Hermit (1.5

km) and the church of the Panaghia. Signs in the village also take you to the church of the Panaghia, a beautifully restored single-aisle church built on a hill of cypress trees. The large village of Spilia is beautiful and very green. You leave Spilia and drive north to meet with the national road at Kolymbari. From there you head west towards Chania.

KASTELLI
ELAFONISSI
KASTELLI

You set out from Chania on the national road towards Kastelli Kissamou. When you reach the 36th kilometer

point of the route, turn left towards Koleni. After 1 kilometer you will see a right turn to Kissamos and *Elafonissi* (44 km), which you take. Drapanias is 1 kilometer away. Follow the signs on the rural road leading to the Minoan and Classical settlements. Drapanias is a large village featuring many surviving Venetian dwellings. You leave Drapanias and arrive in **Kaloudiana,** 2 kilometers away. Turn left inside the village for *Topolia* (8 km) and *Elafonissi* (40 km). 3 kilometers later you arrive in the village of **Potamida** (43rd kilometer point). Like most roadside villages,

Potamida has been built up over the years and now contains mostly modern structures of no particular interest. 2 kilometers south of Potamida is the village of **Voulgaro** (45th km). Here you will want to make a brief detour to visit some sights of exceptional cultural and environmental interest. Upon exiting the village you turn left towards Mouri and **Latziana**. You proceed down a rural road through the olive trees and descend into a ravine. 3 kilometers later you arrive at a small chapel. Leave your car here and descend the ravine on foot to see the ruins of the large church of *Aghia Varvara*, which was the *katholikon* or main church of a

monastery and dates from the second half of the 11th century. Scattered around the site you will see ancient architectural fragments, some of which were utilized in the construction of the church. Continue north along the rural road. There is a wonderful view at this point of the other side of the valley and countless olive trees.

There is also a clear view of Topolia and the Topoliano Gorge, the Cretan Sea and Kastelli. The particularly breathtaking view is of the church of *Aghios Antonios*, which is built on the north edge of a hill, wedged between two ravines that form its vertical walls on the east, west and north. We highly recommend the route from Voulgaro-Latziana-Aghia Varvara-

Aghios Antonios along the rural road and between the two gorges. With Aghios Antonios and the panoramic view behind you, you continue south along the rural road. 200 meters later you reach the Byzantine church of *Aghios Nikolaos*, which dates from 12th/13th century and is a very rare architectural type for Crete. After this detour (total 4 km) in the village of Voulgaro, you return to the main road and resume driving south. After 3 kilometers (48th) you arrive in **Topolia**, a large village whose main attraction is the gorge of the same name. The main road runs along the side of the 1500-meter

134

long gorge. On the slope to the right of the exit is the cave of Aghia Irini. Just below is the village of **Koutsomatado**, which has taverns, parking, and rooms to let. The village is built in the ravine at the exit of the Topolia Gorge, and the route beyond it goes through a plane tree forest and is extremely picturesque. 3 kilometers further is the village of Myloi and the crossroads for *Vlato* (1 km) and the traditional settlement of *Milia* (6.5 km). At the exit of the same village is another intersection towards *Strovles* (2 km), *Paleohora* and *Kantanos*, *Vouta* (19 km), *Chrysoskalitissa* (19 km) and *Elafonissi* (15 km). You continue on the road to Chrysoskalitissa. After 4 kilometers you arrive at the village of **Elos**, which is built in a ravine filled with chestnut and plane trees. The village is known for its honey, and there is a rest stop at the exit. At a place called the Oasis you will find natural drinking water and shady plane trees. The name Elos, meaning marshland, obviously comes from the

area's abundant water. Beginning here, the road narrows and is full of bends (drive carefully!) but the landscape is truly magnificent with its olive trees, chestnut trees and arbutus. 2 kilometers past the intersection (67ᵗʰ) you arrive at the village of **Vathi formerly known as Kouneni**. Vathi is one of the Ennea Horia (Municipality of Inahorion) and has many

AGHIOS GEORGIOS

Byzantine churches. Park your car here and continue on foot. Turn right onto a small paved road. Just beyond are the churches of Aghios Georgios and Aghios Ioannis Chrystostomos. The Catholic Church of Santa Maria is in the field on the left as you enter the village (there is no sign so it is rather difficult to spot). 1 kilometer past Vathi is the very picturesque but abandoned village of **Plokamiana**. Note that the entire route from the crossroads to

PLOKAMIANA

CHRYSOSKALITISSA

Chrysoskalitissa is part of the **E4** route, distinguished for its extraordinary natural beauty. The route passes through a gorge, runs adjacent to a riverbank and the region is a wildlife sanctuary. The riverbank you drive along has a pine forest. You are nearing the sea and the area of Chrysoskalitissa, which has gypsum quarries. At the 74ᵗʰ kilometer point of the

ELAFONISSI

drive you arrive at **Chrysoskalitissa Monastery**. After visiting the monastery you continue on the road to **Elafonissi**, which is 6 kilometers further south. This place on the southwestern end of Crete is worth the trip for the unique beach with its fine white sand, turquoise water, the

island that you reach on foot (!), the tamarisks, the thyme and the cedar trees. You leave Elafonissi and, 1 kilometer later, turn right on a road that starts out as asphalt but soon becomes dirt and takes you to the area's famed cedar forest. Proceed straight and then right towards the sea. The cedar forest is not visible from the road at any point. It is next to the sea and you must stop your car and walk in order to view it from above. After Elafonissi

you resume driving on the main road. 14 kilometers later you come to an intersection. Take the right to *Chania* (79 km), *Kastelli* (41 km) and *Kefali*. 200 meters beyond is **Kefali**, a picturesque village built on the slope with a spectacular view of the gorge that ends at Elafonissi, and of Chrysoskalitissa. There are many shops and

hotels. The village contains the painted Byzantine church of the Metamorphosis (Transfiguration) and the church of Aghios Athanassios near the grammar school. You

continue driving through Kefali in order to return to Kastelli on Crete's westernmost artery, which is also part of the **E4** trail. 2 kilometers further is the hillside

village of **Papadiana** with a marvelous view of the gorge and beautiful stone houses. 2 more kilometers and you arrive at **Simantiriana**, another small, picturesque village built on the side of a mountain and the southernmost village of Crete's westernmost artery. At this point you begin your drive back up north. 3 kilometers bring you to **Amygdalokefali**, an abandoned but still beautiful hill village with a view of the west coast. This portion of the trip is truly lovely at high

altitude. Although it has numerous bends, the road is a good one and takes you through many mountain villages with views of the west coast. After 2 kilometers you go through **Keramoti**. 1 kilometer further is the left turn to *Livadia* (4.5). 4 kilometers later you arrive in **Kambos**, a large village with many homes, shops, restaurants, natural beauty and many arbutus trees. The road out of Kambos runs alongside a ravine that nature lovers will find fascinating. Just opposite the ravine is the other, quite isolated settlement of the village. In the village you will find footpaths to the village of *Melissia* and the *Sacred Church of Aghios Petros*, and to the traditional settlement of *Milia*. 6 kilometers south of Kambos is **Sfinari**, a large

coastal village with shops and rooms to let. Past Sfinari turn left towards the beach. Here the tomato patches reach practically to the water's edge. There are many greenhouses and a dirt road runs the length of the beach. The beach is pebbly and stand of tamarisks. On the west end of the beach you'll find several fish restaurants and a campground. 8 kilometers north of Sfinari is an intersection that goes right to *Lousakies* (4 km) and left to *Platanos* (1 km). Take the olive-tree-lined narrow road for Lousakies, which also is classified as **E4**. Just beyond the village of Zahariana turn left onto a small asphalt road that takes you to the Byzantine church of the Assumption. The church is cruciform with a dome, but unfortunately has been whitewashed both inside and out, covering over its fresco decoration. The churchyard has an enormous plane tree and has been converted into a refreshment stand. You leave Zahariana and return to the basic route. 1 kilometer after the intersection to Lousakies you pass through the village of **Platanos**, a large village with old and new houses, shops, banks, restaurants, etc. In the village you will find a left turn for **Ancient Falassarna** (**4 km**). After visiting the archeological site and the wonderful beach at Falassarna with its fish restaurants and hotels, you return to Platanos and turn left towards **Kastelli**, 10 kilometers away. After touring the seaside town of Kastelli with its beautiful beach and ruins of a Venetian fortress, you get back on the national road to return to Chania, which is 42 kilometers away.

INDEX

BIBLIOGRAPHY

ANDREADAKI-VLAZAKI MARIA, *The Prefecture of Chania Through its Monuments*, Athens 1996 (Greek)

ANDRIANAKIS MICHALIS, *The Old Town of Chania*, Athens 1997 (Greek)

BASILICATA FRANCESCO, *Cretae Regnum*, 1618 / Greek translation with essays by V. Danezi-Lambrinou, Heraklion 1994

VOLONAKIS I., "The Early Christian Monuments of Crete", *Kritika Hronika 1987*, pp. 235-261 (Greek)

CORNELIUS FLAM., *Creta Sacra*, Vol. I-II, Venetiis 1755

GALLAS, WESSEL, BORBOUDAKIS, *Byzantinisches Kreta*, München 1983

Crete: History and Culture, Association of United Municipalities & Communities, Crete 1988 (Greek)

GEROLA GUISEPPE, *Monumenti Veneti nell isola di Creta*, Vol. I-IV, Venezia MCMIII-MCMXXXII-X

GRYNTAKIS YANNIS, *The Conquest of Western Crete by the Turks*, Rethymnon 1998 (Greek)

KARPODINI-DIMITRIADI E., *Castles and Fortresses of Crete*, Athens 1995 (Greek)

PASHLEY ROBERT, *Travels in Crete*, Vol I-II, London 1837

PLATON N., "Wood-roofed Early Christian Basilicas of Crete", *Minutes of Eighth International Byzantine Conference*, Thessaloniki 1953, Vol. A. (Athens 1955), pp. 415-430 (Greek)

PSILAKIS NIKOS, *The Monasteries of Crete*, 1986 (Greek)

POCOCKE RICHARD, *A Description of the East and Some other Countries*, London 1745

SCOTT C. R., *Travels in Crete* (An unknown journey of 1834), Comments and Greek translation G.P. Ekkekakis, Rethymnon 1995

SPANAKIS STERGIOS, *Crete, a guide*, Vol. 2, Heraklion 1969 (Greek)

SPANAKIS STERGIOS, *Cities and Villages of Crete*, Heraklion 1991 (Greek)

SPRATT T.A.B., *Travels and Researches in Crete by Captain T.A.B. Spratt*, Vol 1-2, London 1865

TOURNEFORT JOSEPH PITTON DE, *Relation d' un voyage du Levant*, Paris 1717

TSIVIS YANNIS, *Chania 1252-1940*, Athens 1993 (Greek)

TSOUGARAKIS D., *Byzantine Crete, From the 5th Century to the Venetian Conquest*, Athens 1988

ZACHARIS ASTERIOS, *National Park, The Samarian Gorge* (Greek)